A GUIDE TO CARE AND GROW NATURAL HAIR
&
IT'S CONNECTION TO YOUR HEALTH AND WEALTH

Desreta Jackson

Edited by Eve Parker
Cover Design by Creative Genius

Printed in USA by Black Beauty LLC
751 S. Weir Canyon Rd. Ste 157-1024
Anaheim Hills, CA 92808

Table of Contents

Acknowledgments 5

Introduction 7

Chapter 1: What Inspired This Book **9**

    Here Hair 11

Chapter 2: A Conspiracy, A Coincidence, Or More? **17**

    The Hair Conspiracy 19

    The Black Hair Conspiracy 23

Chapter 3: Understand Your Past **27**

    Legacy 29

    Significance of Hair in Different Cultures 36

Chapter 4: Understanding the Element **41**

    Understanding Why Hair Grows 43

    What is Your Hair Type? 45

Chapter 5: Intentions **47**

    The BlackSilk Technique 49

    Step by Step 51

Chapter 6: The Plan **55**

    The Plan 57

    1st Month 60

    2nd Month 62

    3rd Month 64

4th Month.. 66

5th Month.. 68

6th Month.. 70

7th Month.. 72

8th Month.. 74

9th Month.. 76

10th Month.. 78

11th Month.. 80

12th Month.. 82

Chapter 7: Shampooing.. 85

Shampooing... 87

Chapter 8: Conditioning 91

Conditioning 93

Chapter 9: Offense Defense 97

The Clear Protector 99

Hair Greases and Oils 102

Chapter 10: Sulfate-Free vs. Sulfate............................ 105

Sulfate- free vs. Sulfate 107

Cradle Cap... 109

Dandruff...110

Ringworm of the Scalp 112

Traction Alopecia 114

Chapter 11: The Truth About Vitamins.......................... 117

The Truth About Vitamins..119

Chapter 12: How To Care For Her 121

Trimming Your Hair.. 123

Chapter 13: The Perceptions of Braids and Weaves............ 127

Braids and Weaves 129

Combs and Brushes 134

Chapter 14: Good Hair VS. Bad Hair **137**

Good Hair vs. Bad Hair... 139

Chapter 15: The Willie Lynch Letter........................ **141**

The Willie Lynch Letter 143

Chapter 16: Lies Mama Told **145**

The Top Five Myths Revealed 147

Home Remedy Tips 151

Chapter 17: Your Hair's Connection to The Universe **153**

Your Hair's Connection to the Universe 155

Chapter 18: Match the Frequency **161**

Are You Negative or Positive?..................................... 163

Chapter 19: Topics and Questions Discussion **169**

Topics and Questions... 171

How to Order BlackSilk Products 172

Bibliography.. 173

Acknowledgments

I dedicate this book to the people who have helped or influenced its creation. **Dawn Lee** my cousin, R.I.P. As a little girl, there has to be a braider in your life that you are able to watch to learn how to braid hair. Out of all my teen cousins at the time she was the only one who cared to consistently comb and style my hair, always trying to pick up those little ends to help them grow. I would look up at her as I sat between her legs and think to myself how wonderful and beautiful she was for always making me feel like I mattered in a world that tried to keep telling me I didn't.

To my kids Adam, Eve and King, I would be lost in this would without you guys. You gave me my reason for survival and drive. I find myself missing a big piece of my heart whenever you guys are away to long from me. For our journey in life will always be connected. Each one of you have helped me in one way or another with this book from my son Adam and his reassurance of my inner belief to help encourage me to continue writing over the years and my daughter Eve who not only edited and help format the book. I appreciate and love you all.

My husband **Darryl Battle** for giving me that special push in 2009 when I became pregnant with our son and he saw how the pregnancy was draining me and that I was not able to multi-task or be as productive as much as I wanted. He held me late one night and said, "I know it is killing you not to do all the things you used to, but maybe everything happened for a reason. Why don't you write that book you been telling me about from when we first met?" You are my number one fan, my knight in shinning armor and my shoulder to cry on when I need it. Thank you King!

I love each one of you and thank you.

To my sister Christalyn Martin you are the epitome of what a sister should be. A supporter of your dreams and inspiration in your life and a ride or die. I love you and thank you for having my back at all times.

Introduction

*D*esreta Jackson, born in Tortola, British Virgin Islands, is best known for her starring role as "young Celie" in the 1985 Oscar-nominated film, *The Color Purple*, directed by Steven Spielberg starring Oprah Winfrey, Whoopi Goldberg, Danny Glover and Laurence Fishburne.

Her stellar performance in *The Color Purple* launched her career landing her roles in *Sister Act, Mancuso FBI,* and other made-for-TV movies. It also led to Ms. Jackson producing one of the first reality shows made for television, setting a trend before reality shows became the accepted norm.

Among many other accomplishments, Ms. Jackson was honored with the 2011 Prestige Award for her contribution to African-American history, being honorably cited in the African-American Film Encyclopedia as an iconic actress in cinematic history. She was also honored with not one but two prestigious MAC Awards by the state of Virginia for Black History Month (the VaBHMA). She was the guest of honor being recognized for her philanthropy in the black community and entrepreneurship along with the BULLDOG award for her devotion and perseverance to overcome obstacles. These awards are given only to those who have personally and professionally advocated a future of racial freedom and equality to keep the "Yes We Can" dream alive.

DesretaJackson.com
Facebook / IG/ Twitter : @DesretaJackson

CHAPTER 1

What Inspired This Book

"The Hair Conspiracy is that they know the science and physics behind your hair—they don't want you to know its power. That is why they spread the misinformation about our hair and push us to believe it's just a superficial trend; that it's just hair."
~ Desreta Jackson

Here Hair

I am a professional braider who opened the very first legalized home-based braidery in 2001 and I have been doing hair professionally for over 25 years. I am also known as the child actress who starred in the historical black film, *The Color Purple*, playing the role of young Celie, who ironically was known for those nappy pigtail braids. Those who know me have even wondered if that contributed to my fascination with hair. It didn't. I grew up in the Virgin Islands amongst a culture of braiders. Unlike the U.S. where there are convenience stores on every corner and doctors were readily available; our herbs were our medicine. There were bakers who we trade and bartered our goods with. Understanding essential oils and the healing properties of nature was common knowledge. I didn't expect this knowledge to become of such value to me later in life.

I was also no stranger to hair care and braids. Those pigtails I wore in the film were very real for me before and after *The Color Purple*. Every morning when I was in middle school, my hair would be in plaits, but by the time I got to school, I would take them out and redo my own hair out of embarrassment. You see, on the island such a look was very common and readily accepted, but after we moved to the United States I soon discovered that the 'norm' for hairstyles and hair care was quite different.

Nonetheless, I firmly believe that it is our life experiences and everything we encounter that helps build our character and determine our life's path. I understood even back then the value of a dollar and wanted to invest my acting earnings into something more. That led to me successfully running my first business as a teenager with the help and guidance of my mother. My first business, a beauty supply store, located in Watts, California on the corner of Manchester Ave. and Avalon. It was one of the only few black-owned beauty salons around at the time. My investment was paying off well. I was fully stocked and had a well-diversified inventory. Since I was an emancipated minor at the age of 16, I could move gracefully into business deals without the standard limitations for most minors. I even had my own braidery set up in the back of the store where I did hair for a lengthy list of clientele. This ended with a bitter tale because I eventually had to close my doors as I was a victim of the infamous Rodney King Riots in 1992. For those who are not familiar with this historic incident, Wikipedia describes it as the following:

> *The 1992 Los Angeles riots, also known as the Rodney King riots, the South Central riots, the 1992 Los Angeles civil disturbance, the 1992 Los Angeles civil unrest, and the Los Angeles uprising, were a series of riots, lootings, arsons, and civil disturbance that occurred in Los Angeles County, California, in 1992. The riot started in South Central Los Angeles and then spread out into other areas over a six-day period within the Los Angeles metropolitan area in California, beginning in April 1992. The riots started on April 29 after a trial jury acquitted four police officers of the Los Angeles Police Department of the use of excessive force in the videotaped arrest and beating of Rodney King, following a high-speed police chase. Thousands of people throughout the metropolitan area in Los Angeles rioted over six days following the announcement of the verdict.*
>
> *Widespread looting, assault, arson, and killings occurred during the riots, and estimates of property damage was over $1 billion. The rioting ended after members of the California Army National Guard, the 7th Infantry Division, and the 1st Marine Division were called in to stop the rioting when the local police could not control the situation. In total, 55 people were killed during the riots and over 2,000 people were injured.*

Going through the LA Riots first hand as a teenager and a business owner who lost everything was mind blowing and Wikipedia can't describe that! I watched as the neighborhood I grew up in, did business in, fought and raised my kids in changed right in front of my eyes. Yes, there was massive looting and burning, yet in the hood, most people didn't know who was doing all the burning. That alone was always strange but other things were too. For example, my area was known as West Los Angeles, but I would watch the nightly news reports try and describe what was happening with all the looting and burning and they'd refer to us as "South Central Los Angeles". Then, in the same year—boom! The film named *South Central* debuted with a horrific portrayal of my neighborhood which, I would like to add, was vastly different from the day to day of what I knew and grew up in. Then I watched my neighborhood diminish as a community. Many people who ran black-owned businesses, lived and grew up in the community, lost their livelihood then their cars and homes, and the crime rate rose dramatically. Many business owners like myself were promised help from organizations but few received it. I couldn't get a loan from anywhere and when I started to reopen the second store some suppliers would play games and would not give me the products I needed to sell. Many other beauty shop owners I personally knew had the same story to tell that I did. I started seeing brand new competitive beauty supply stores being built next door to me or on the same lots with brand new shopping malls. They were mega stores with products and hair supplies that spanned a whole store wall and here I was just trying to get hair grease and running into problems. The purpose of sharing these extra details is for you to understand my in-depth perspective of the hair industry along with my experience.

In 2011, I launched my own hair care line called BlackSilk, "The First African-American Luxury Hair Care Line." As an African-American girl growing up, hair has always been very relevant in my life, but it wasn't until I was pregnant with my little girl that the desire brewed in me to understand why and how black hair grows. So, I took some science classes and tried to find books on the subject, but it was disappointing when I realized there wasn't much out there. The books I found were filled with all of this unnecessary scientific data that still didn't tell me plainly and simply how to grow my little girl's hair. Then, I found a whole new era of books written by women who were born with naturally long or curly hair talking about how to grow and care for their hair. The problem with that was, if you were born with hair genes that naturally allowed your hair to grow long are you truly sharing or teaching something others can emulate? I think not. Unless I came from your mom and dad, I won't have your hair genes.

I found that some of these books were written by men or women of various nationalities and most had no experience with a variety of hair types besides what they had read in books and the only thing they had going for them was a Ph.D. which is an incredible accomplishment to obtain. But before there were schools to give us degrees and tell us the standard to obtain their credentials, there were just people like you and me who had a passion and drive to find the answers on their own. I noticed that none of these books communicated the personal experience to accompany their research. Many of the books were not even written by African-Americans, they just used a picture of an African-American on the cover. None of the books told me step-by-step how to accumulate and maintain length or about their methods and reasoning.

I have intensively researched this matter for over fourteen years interviewing over 5,000 people and experimenting and perfecting my findings through personal results and my clients' personal experiences to master what I call the "BlackSilk Technique" for healthy hair growth. I have found that not just the products you use but also the way you care for your hair can not only increase or decrease your hair growth but is connected to better physical and mental health. This book has been designed to give you a clear and simple definition to tell you when, how and why you should do each step. It does not have to be read page by page and it can also be used as a reference guide for specific problem areas.

Over twenty plus years of doing hair from all over the world and I found myself dedicating these past 10 years to making products that only heal, protect, or help to grow the hair. This has led me to a revelation: hair is more than just for protecting the skin or for beautifying our physical appearance. I irrefutably believe that hair in and of itself serves a greater purpose. It's more than just hair.

In this book, I intend to educate, uplift and clear up some of our urban myths about our hair. This book is not just for African-Americans, blacks, mixed- race or whatever title you identify as but for anyone who would like a more in-depth understanding of a hidden culture whose traditions and behaviors have been widely misunderstood for a very long time. To understand this hidden information, you must first understand the science and physics behind the origin of hair.

When considering how our solar system was born and created, many scientists believe that the solar system was formed when a cloud of gas and dust in space was disturbed, by the possible explosion of a nearby star (called a supernova). This explosion made waves in space which squeezed the cloud of gas and dust. This gas cloud composed mostly of gases, such as hydrogen and helium, formed our large planet. This information is relevant because the chemical makeup of our hair is mainly keratin which is composed of the elements: carbon, oxygen, hydrogen, nitrogen, and sulfur. These elements that are also found in space are the most commonly found elements in living organisms. Thus, our hair contains the elements for life.

The hair itself harnesses the energy directly from the sun. This energy possesses great power that is directly connected to our health if we understand how to utilize its power we can not only help to enhance our health but find better financial wealth for ourselves! To begin understanding and controlling the energy and power of our hair, I purpose this formula: Understand your past, understand the element, learn the intentions behind your products, identify the truths and lies, meditate for your hair, and match the frequency.

CHAPTER 2

A Conspiracy, A Coincidence, Or More?

"They want you to think it is just hair because then you will treat it with less care."
~ Desreta Jackson

The Hair Conspiracy

*C*ontrary to what we may believe, there is a Hair Conspiracy and most of us have fallen victim to it. The color of your hair has been subjected to discrimination and misinformation just as much as your skin or gender. If your hair is the color black it's considered to be a lower social ranking than if it was blond or red; but, science actual says black hair color is more valuable than any other hair color based on the universal law for energy. This is due to melanin, the pigment in hair that makes it appear black or brown, being light sensitive and able to be used as a conductor. Yet, we are conditioned to believe that black hair color is boring and mundane. It is far from both. Somewhere, in this life journey, we have become disoriented from the instincts that tell us what is true, and what is false. We are fed a daily dose of propaganda from television, radio, magazines and blogs in the mass media.

I wrote this book with the intent to help educate, guide and uplift people who may not feel comfortable with the current information or perception they have been given about their hair; especially those whose hair is the color black. You may have been a victim of The Black Hair Conspiracy. I believe we are all part of a wonderful human race and education of our cultural differences and DNA makeup can only help us to grow as a people. So, with that said whether you are from Russia, France, China, Africa or a mixture of multiple backgrounds; you need this book. Whether for yourself or maybe your offspring, or perhaps for just a general understanding of culture and hair. In order for you to understand anything, you must always understand its ROOTS!

I have always been a fan of cultural differences and intrigued with the beauty and diversity we have in clothing, habits, hair, etc. Because of this interest, I have seen many cultures ridiculed for not practicing their traditional hair care or beliefs, and without a strong mental personal belief, many descendants lose their way. My belief is that we lose our way and get distracted easily into a wormhole because we don't truly understand the roots of the propaganda we are being fed.

I have consistently seen evidence that there is indeed a hair conspiracy and more importantly a black hair conspiracy. Many industries would like you to believe that your hair is mainly about fashion and fashion trends, that way you will be subject to manipulation and propaganda concerning what to buy, how to wear it, how to style it, what is hot and what is not! But, hair is so much more. There is a spiritual, health, and inner and outer planetary connection to the universe and the way money flows within. Its connected with the universe and what God or a higher self has planned for you. In order for you to understand yourself, your true calling, or your inner power you must first look within to discover who you are now. If you ask the right questions, it will help connect you to your past ancestors and your current health status.

What are the right questions you ask? Well, stand in front of the mirror. Now describe five things about your hair. As for me my hair is black, has very tight curls, is extremely shiny, curly when wet, and not very soft to the touch but not unpleasantly hard. This tells me five things. I am a black woman. I have a set pattern for how I like things done but I am flexible. I am considered a shining star. I know how to have fun when it's time. Lastly, I am a very loving person, but I can give a hard exterior. This look within myself tells me of my ancestry. I am a descendant of a black race of people with a strong background of fighters and loving people. They most likely had to be able to be versatile for the situation.

One of the more interesting and newer concept I've seen develop is the birth of all-natural hair products. Personally, I love the idea and have always been an advocate of home remedies or natural ways to solve problems. However, keep in mind that even though Mother Nature produces natural chemicals, these too can be very dangerous if we do not understand how to properly use them and their limits.

Recently, a young lady approached me at one of my conferences and wanted to know if Sulfate was truly as bad as they said. I told her before I give you my opinion let me give you added information and facts and then you can be the judge. First, understand that shampoos have been in use since the 1800s but at first people simply used bars of soap to wash their hair. It was not until around the 20th century that shampoos, like what we know of today, were introduced in a liquid form. In 1930, Procter & Gamble created the first liquid shampoo that had a sulfate base and that changed the game. It was so thorough in how it cleaned the hair that it transformed the hair care industry altogether and a bottle of it still sits in the Smithsonian Museum today.

Now since the 1930s, we have been using products with sulfate and with great success, I might add. In 2000, a shampoo company produced an organic-based shampoo on the market and started to promote sulfate-free shampoos and share information on the drawbacks of sulfate in shampoos. It was rumored that they needed to come up with a marketing strategy to get people to buy and notice their products but in the process of starting a Sulfate-Free campaign. They were sued and although their campaign did spread initially, no one has heard much of the company since. Additionally, as I went to research the company for this book I couldn't seem to find any information on the company or any information on the lawsuit anymore. Therefore, this is just a rumor and I have no proof to support this claim. However, out of this initial Sulfate-free campaign came the amazing birth of additional natural products and a nation of people who wanted to become more natural.

The Hair Conspiracy was born out of greed and mass marketing. It has been derived from the same concept as what I would call the Beauty Conspiracy, which tries to teach women that they are always in need of improving their looks. It sells the belief that buying certain products women can achieve this level of beauty which will equate to them feeling beautiful. I feel like the hair care industry has taken part in this by promoting the idea that your hair is superficial and only a fashion statement. This idea is not only a contradiction but also a double standard. Outlets such as magazines and hair shows push hair as only a fashion statement. Yet, African-Americans are told it's just hair and simultaneously must endure mandatory hair requirements for employment.

I had to ask myself one day, how did we get so confused and misled that we know so little about our own hair which we are born with and spend all our lives with? Then I noticed when I would travel to non-westernized lands that they are very connected to their hair roots and customs. Yes, you may have a few here and there that try to Americanize themselves but generally, the people are well connected to its cultural history. Many even have their own ancient hair secrets, oils, and styling rituals for their own hair and hair type. It is not until you come to the United States that it seems as if everything is mixed-up or combined. Yes, we are a great nation, a melting pot of nationalities and cultures. Maybe somehow, we are adapting to the change by integrating and maybe even subconsciously interweaving American Culture into our native lands. Remember many came from all over the world like Ireland, Russia, Africa, Asia and so on…all bringing their rich history, customs and hair rituals, and beliefs. As our beautiful country developed and grew, some of these cultures spread and became unknowingly apart of the roots or branches of other cultures such as mine. I am from the British Virgin Islands and there is a saying that is known well in my homeland. The phrase is *piss poor*. In a sentence it might be used as such: you are so piss poor you don't have a pot to piss in or a window to throw it out. But, the truth is that statement that didn't originate in the British Virgin Islands, it is derived from the United States, during the settlers' time many people were told to "go west" for land. Unfortunately, many found nothing but poor land to live on and no work. They were so poor that some would get a pot and collect the family's daily urine and at the end of the day sell it. At the time they would use the urine to dye hides, therefore, it was useful and profitable, but some families were so poor they couldn't afford to buy a tin pot. Hence the phrase *piss poor*. The interesting thing is many American children are not familiar with this phrasing and yet it is more a part of their culture than mine.

This story clearly illustrates the cultural assimilation of both language and customs. Therefore, I maintain a firm belief that because for centuries now, the wonderful and great country of the United States has been comprised of a melting pot of different cultures coming together, the U.S. was not able to give birth to a cultural ritual of its own concerning hair.

The Hair Conspiracy is that they know the science and physics behind your hair—they don't want you to know its power. That is why they spread the misinformation about our hair and push us to believe it's just a superficial trend; that it's just hair.

The Black Hair Conspiracy

*I*n community college, I studied Philosophy, one of my favorite subjects back then. I had mixed feelings about the biologist, Charles Darwin, and some of his beliefs and what he preached and said during his lifetime, but as we all know many of his beliefs built a nation of believers and quotes.

Despite his theories being used against African-Americans, understand this—if you are here today you are grand and greatly endowed with all of the dominant and/or superior traits of your ancestors. I support this fact by reminding you of *Darwin's Theory of Evolution.* Charles Darwin's proven hypothesis simply brought something new called, *natural selection.*

What is natural selection? Well, according to Darwin's extensive research, natural selection acts to preserve and accumulate minor advantages in genetic mutations. For example, a member of a species developed a functional advantage (adaptation) like growing wings, then they will learn to fly and all their offspring would inherit that advantage and pass it on to their offspring. Due to the demands of the natural terrain of our ancestors in Egypt and Africa, being forcibly made into slaves, we had to adapt to unbelievable standards, developing certain traits to ensure our survival.

In Darwin's Theory, it is noted that, over time, the inferior, disadvantaged members of the same species that had more recessive traits would gradually die out, leaving only the superior (advantaged) members of the species to live and pass on these traits to future offspring.

Therefore, natural selection can be seen as the preservation of a functional advantage that enables a species to compete better in the wild. Natural selection is the natural equivalent to domestic breeding. As unearthed by archeologists, ancient Egyptians were more than likely the oldest civilization documented to practice the domestication and animal husbandry of various animals. Through this refined art, human breeders, over several thousands of years, have produced dramatic changes in domestic animal populations by selecting individuals of a species to breed.

This practice of "domestication" did not stop with animals, as it was extended in inhumane ways to human beings, beginning with the Portuguese and their African captives, during the Trans-Atlantic Slave trade in 1555, spreading to the shores of North America, where slave owners would, through "slave breeding" practices, pick the strongest, most desired male slaves to impregnate their specially selected female slaves.

Breeders eliminate undesirable traits gradually over the course of time, focusing on what would be a benefit for them and couple their animals according to this advantage. Similarly, natural selection eliminates inferior species gradually over time.

This natural selection process is seen in human beings as differentiating various traits that are either "dominant" or "recessive." This is seen in the texture or color of hair, skin, eyes and other characteristics.

The Hair Conspiracy has manipulated these genetic characteristics, stereotyping differences in hair color and texture. We use terms such as good hair or bad hair; as if your hair has committed a criminal act that has to be punished because it is not tamed. During the enslavement of African women, they were forbidden by law to wear their hair in cultural styles. The belief was it would help prevent the French and English men from finding the African women attractive. When this didn't work they were ordered to wear rags on their heads. Oh, did you think we did this to protect our hair from damage—my bad, another black hair conspiracy.

How much has changed since then? On October 24, 2013, The Huffington Post, a widely known and respected online newspaper shared an article titled, "Company Policy Requires Missouri Woman to Cut Her Dreadlocks to Keep Her Job." The article reads:

> *Ashley Davis, a 24-year-old from St. Peters, Missouri,*
> *said a change in her company's policy now requires her to*
> *cut off her dreadlocks. "I've only been there for two months,*

*and they came up with a policy. I feel like it's degrading,"
she said.*

*According to Fox 2 St. Louis, the policy was imple-
mented on September 21st-- a few weeks after Davis began working there. The policy states, "dreadlocks, braids,
Mohawks, mullets and other such hairstyles are against
company guidelines."*

Davis tells the local Fox station she had the dreadlocks when they
hired her, and she's been growing her locks for ten years. To her, they're
apart of her culture and everyone in her family wears them. But she's the
only one in her office who wears the hairstyle.

Then two years later on Septembers 24, 2015 The Huffington Post
shared another article about the banning of black hairstyles. The head-
line read: "The Lorain Horizon Science Academy in Ohio is facing heat
from the natural hair community after a copy of a letter to parents that
included a ban on Afro puffs and 'small twisted braids'."

Around the 1400s, when African slaves were brought west to the
"New World," they were confronted with their first loss of identity. It was
not accidental that the Black Conspiracy (as I call it) eroded our pride
and culture. In the late 1700s, there was a law passed under the admin-
istration of Governor Esteban Rodriguez Miro called the Tignon Law.
This law required women of African descent to cover their hair so that
they would not attract the French and Spanish Creole men. For many
of the women of African descent were getting too much attention and it
was already widely known that they were established as a favorite of the
men as mistresses. In hopes of stopping the men from being so attracted
to the African women, the law was passed to have them to cover their
hair with a knotted headdress. This was intended to mark the women
as inferior to the white women, but it had backfired in a dramatic turn
of events. In fact, our creative and intuitive skills came through as the
African women would start using bright red and blue decorative ribbons
and fancy tying knots to their head scarfs and quickly it became a fashion statement and movement. It was then that the one and only identity
they had, was stripped from them. The standards of beauty that they
saw were the slave masters who called themselves superior with their

fair skin and straight hair vs. all those they saw being treated badly and called inferior, people of their own image with dark skin and kinky hair.

Now over the years Africans and African-Americas have embraced the European standards of beauty and hairstyles as a required way of surviving and living, even making some of these standards our own.

We have now created our own artistry to create styles and standards that reflect a unique and creative black culture. We should be proud of how we have mutated to evolve no matter if we wear weaves sometimes, our own naturally curly hair, braids, or any other creative styles. We own them all and should shout from the mountaintop that we are the originators, creators, and inventors of our own hairstyles and creations.

"What is important to me isn't who I am or what I have done, as much as being able to trace my lineage and what I can contribute to my legacy is."
~ Desreta Jackson

CHAPTER 3

Understand Your Past

"Energy cannot be created or destroyed."
~ Albert Einstein

Legacy

nderstanding your personal cultural background is the first step to understanding and controlling the power of hair. They say if you don't know your history it will repeat itself. Therefore, I use this as the guideline for me. For me, I am African American with a West Indian cultural background. I spent a lot of time running from island to island with my mother (who always told us that we had to run away from my father because he was trying to kidnap and sell me). This led to us having to survive on many different islands. Thus, I was never able to accumulate or bring along any possessions that held monetary value. The only thing I was able to bring was knowledge of my island culture. Such as making red beans and rice or walking up the hills to pick up my favorite snack, blood pudding.

At the age of 9, I came to the U.S. with nothing. Although, I didn't have heirlooms or items to be passed down to my children; I had core values of my culture, memories of food and experiences to share with them. That became a part of my legacy. This made me realize that legacy doesn't have to be something tangible to pass down to your children; it can also be something spiritually, mentally, or emotionally. It actually can be good, or it could be bad. I use this to defy what the word legacy means to me.

What is the dictionary definition of the word legacy? Webster's definition: A gift by Will especially of money or other personal property or to something transmitted by or received from an ancestor or predecessor or from the past.

So, it wasn't a surprise to me after really understanding what the word legacy meant, why so many African-Americans were leaving behind a legacy that was not of their ancestors but of their oppressors. There was never any monetary restitution given after hundreds of years of slavery. Therefore, it was very unlikely that you're going to pass down any heirlooms of any value. The promised compensation of forty acres and a mule has become a symbolic phrase used over time. Instead of becoming anything of financial value that we can pass down (such as land or jewelry) it has become just a joke.

Have you ever wondered where the saying forty acres and a mule came from? Well, it refers to a concept in the United States for agrarian reform for enslaved African-American farmers, post the harsh and cruel institution of slavery. Many freed slaves believed and were told by those in power, like political figures, that they had a right to own the land they had long worked on as slaves and expected to legally claim forty acres of land and a mule after the end of the American Civil War. This belief is due to a request and promise by General William Tecumseh Sherman of the American Civil War. The General needed more men to fight in the war and made a deal with the African-American pastors in the community. He asked the pastors to convince more African-American men to fight and in return, he would reward the soldiers with 40 acres.

Now, for you to understand the severity of this promise let me explain why it was called Sherman's Special Field Order and why our ancestors believed in this promise. General William Tecumseh Sherman, commander of the Military Division of the Mississippi of the United States Army had control of 400,000 acres (1,600 km2) of land along the Atlantic coast of South Carolina, Georgia, and Florida that were set to be divided into parcels of not more than 40 acres.

General William T. Sherman

Take a look at a copy of the actual order from *Memoirs of Gen. William T. Sherman* - Volume 2 by William Tecumseh Sherman below and notice section IV.

Special Field Orders No. 15.

Special Field Orders No. 15.

Headquarters Military Division of the Mississippi,
In the Field, Savannah, Ga., January 16, 1865.

I.   The islands from Charleston south, the abandoned rice-fields along the rivers for thirty miles back from the sea, and the country bordering the Saint Johns River, Fla., are reserved and set apart for the settlement of the BLACKS now made free by the acts of war and the proclamation of the President of the United States.

II. At Beaufort, Hilton Head, Savannah, Fernandina, Saint Augustine, and Jacksonville the blacks may remain in their chosen or accustomed vocations; but on the islands, and in the settlements hereafter to be established, no white person whatever, unless military officers and soldiers detailed for duty, will

---

be permitted to reside; and the sole and exclusive management of affairs will be left to the freed people themselves, subject only to the United States military authority and the acts of Congress. By the laws of war and orders of the President of the United States the negro is free, and must be dealt with as such. He cannot be subjected to conscription or forced military service, save by the written orders of the highest military authority of the Department, under such regulations as the President or Congress may prescribe; domestic servants, blacksmiths, carpenters, and other mechanics will be free to select their own work and residence, but the young and able-bodied negroes must be encouraged to enlist as soldiers in the service of the United States, to contribute their share toward maintaining their own freedom and securing their rights as citizens of the United States. Negroes so enlisted will be organized into companies, battalions, and regiments, under the orders of the United States military authorities, and will be paid, fed, and clothed according to law. The bounties paid on enlistment may, with the consent of the recruit, go to assist his family and settlement in procuring agricultural implements, seed, tools, boats, clothing, and other articles necessary for their livelihood.

III. Whenever three respectable negroes, heads of families, shall desire to settle on land, and shall have selected for that purpose an island, or a locality clearly defined within the limits above designated, the inspector of settlements and plantations will himself, or by such sub-ordinate officer as he may appoint, give them a license to settle such island or district, and afford them such assistance as he can to enable them to establish a peaceable agricultural settlement. The three parties named will subdivide the land, under the supervision of the inspector, among themselves and such others as may choose to settle near them, so that each family shall have a plot of not more than forty acres of tillable ground, and when it borders on some water channel with not more than

800 feet water front, in the possession of which land the military authorities will afford them protection until such time as they can protect themselves or until Congress shall regulate their title. The quartermaster may, on the requisition of the inspector of settlements and plantations, place at the disposal of the inspector one or more of the captured steamers to ply between the settlements and one or more of the commercial points, heretofore named in orders, to afford the settlers the opportunity to supply their necessary wants and to sell the products of their land and labor.

IV. Whenever a negro has enlisted in the military service of the United States he may locate his family in any one of the settlements at pleasure and acquire a homestead and all other rights and privileges of a settler as though present in person. In like manner negroes may settle their families and engage on board the gunboats, or in fishing, or in the navigation of the inland waters, without losing any claim to land or other advantages derived from this system. But no one, unless an actual settler as above defined, or unless absent on Government service, will be entitled to claim any right to land or property in any settlement by virtue of these orders.

V. In order to carry out this system of settlement a general officer will be detailed as inspector of settlements and plantations, whose duty it shall be to visit the settlements, to regulate their police and general management, and who will furnish personally to each head of a family, subject to the approval of the President of the United States, a possessory title in writing, giving as near as possible the description of boundaries, and who shall adjust all claims or conflicts that may arise under the same, subject to the like approval, treating such titles altogether as possessory. The same general officer will also be charged with the enlistment and organization of the negro recruits and protecting their interests while absent from their settlements, and will be governed by the rules and regulations prescribed by the War Department for such purpose.

VI. Brig. Gen. R. Saxton is hereby appointed inspector of settlements and plantations and will at once enter on the performance of his duties. No change is intended or desired in the settlement now on Beaufort Island, nor will any rights to property heretofore acquired be affected thereby.

By order of Maj. Gen. W. T. Sherman:
L. N. DAYTON, Assistant Adjutant-General.

—*William T. Sherman, Military Division of the Mississippi; 1865 series - Special Field Order 15, January 16, 1865*

The order was revoked in the fall of that same year by President Andrew Johnson. Then to make matters worse, those who had received their long-promised 40 acres and a mule were thrown from their own land it and the land was repossessed. To this day, African Americans are stilled owed 40 acres and a mule!

Understanding your past allows you to carry the energy of pride and not shame. Both have very powerful energy, but one will lift you up while the other will pull you down. For example, how would you walk into a house when you own it versus breaking into it? How would you carry your posture when you walk around your house when all the bills are paid and the food is in your refrigerator vs, living under someone else's roof and you have no money to contribute to the household? Your posture, your attitude, your energy would all be completely different due to how you feel about yourself and your contributions to the space you occupy. This is why I say you must study and learn your history whether you are Jewish, Italian, Mexican etc. I am African America and learning my historical background was a mind-blowing experience; allowing me to take pride in myself and my ancestry. It has also made me able to recognize that anyone who doesn't allow me to celebrate and take pride in my culture or myself truly doesn't have my best interest at heart. Because loving who I am should not mean that I hate who they are.

> *"Pay attention to who shares happy spirits of your greatest moments with you, who congratulates you, who dismisses you and who ignores you. It does not show you who your friends are, but it will tell you who they are NOT."*
> ~ Desreta Jackson

Significance of Hair in
Different Cultures

*H*air has always been important in every country since history began. Whether your hair is curly or straight is determined by your DNA but its connection to your health has always been there you just didn't know. For example, redheads have been medically proven to be nearly twice as likely to develop Parkinson's disease compared to those with darker hair as sited in Medical Dailey. Many doctors are still not certain why this is. Redheads are also at an increased risk for melanoma, the deadliest form of skin cancer. The MC1R mutation doesn't bind to the PTEN gene, which is known to prevent tumors and safeguard against cancer, according to Harvard Medical School. The US National Library of Medicine reported, that individuals with a light phenotype (i.e., light hair color, light base skin color, and propensity to burn) have more nevi and are at greater risk for developing skin cancer). This implies a great established purpose; our hair is more than just hair and has a bigger purpose in our genetic makeup and survival.

Your hair is directly linked to your mood, health, and financial windfall or downfall. A dying man will choose to put all his money towards saving his life even at the cost of going broke. A sick man will not have a healthy mindset for financial wealth. Have you ever felt down, but after a good hair wash and new hairstyle your mood was lifted? Some even exclaim: "I feel like a million bucks!" As long as you are confined to a mental state that views hair as simply a means to beautify your looks or enhance your sexuality, you will forever be lost on the powers it possesses. You will continue to be fooled by the mainstream market of bad hair products and snake oils designed to take your money. Your hair is the first line of defense and source of your energy. If someone can convince you to cover it, destroy it, or be ashamed of it their battle is half won.

As an African-American, have you ever thought about why hair means so much to us and our offspring? This goes back to our ancestors. For thousands of years, Africans knew no other skin color or hair type but their own. Tribes would create elaborate hairstyles in efforts to outdo each other. This would instill pride along with the identification of other member's tribes, position and wealth.

The Atlantic Slave Trade resulted in the mixing of many different tribes, their placement in the Caribbean to be seasoned, or trained. One of the first things done to them was the shaving of their hair. This was done for physical and psychological effects so that their individuality and pride would be lost. Slaves weren't allowed any hair grooming tools and over time our heritage was lost along with a symbol of our culture.

Therefore, it is not simply by chance that hair has such an essential place in everyday life. It has always been that way throughout the world since the dawn of history, and hair still possesses these amazing attributes even today.

Hair in Chinese Culture

China is one of the most ancient civilizations in the world. Deeply influenced by Confucianism, Chinese traditions in most of its terminology and customs reflect this way of life. This philosophy emphasizes the importance of ancestry. Since very early times, the variety of their hairstyles are some of the most beautiful styles in the world. Chinese culture has given increasing value to the understanding of hair along with its history and a strong symbolic meaning. Their use of haircuts and hairstyles are noticeable and can express social or civil status, religion or profession. As China is a conglomeration of peoples and cultural groups, there are many styles and regional customs. Nevertheless, the significance of hair is prevalent throughout the land.

> *"Our bodies, to every hair and shred of skin, are received from our parents. We must not presume to injure or to wound them. This is the beginning of filial piety.*

When we have established our character by the practice of this filial course, so as to make our name famous in future ages and thereby glorify our parents, this is the end of filial piety."

Confucius, (551-470 BC)

Hair in African and Black Culture

African civilization had a variety of different hairstyles. A lot of people are still wearing many of these, inspiring antique African hairstyles in the world. They are symbolic hairstyles as a result of tribal traditions. Hairstyles in Africa and those worn by African-Americans are ever-changing, yet deeply rooted in a shared past. Hairdressing in Africa is always the work of trusted friends or relatives. In addition to the affable social aspects of the event, the hair, in the hands of an enemy, could become a constituent in the production of a hazardous charm or "medicine" that would harm the owner. Thus, many African cultures regard hair is as having great power and value.

Ask almost any black lady what's her connection with her hair and she will most likely agree that its similar to a having a mate. Whether it's the long-committed hours spent waiting at the hair salon, the pain endured from braiding, or the amount of money spent—hair is actually an infatuation. While I understand other cultures value hair, too, in Black culture hair is tremendously significant and often identical with individuality.

Hair in Jewish Culture

In the high temperatures of summer or the rain of winter, you can tell that a woman is a spiritual conventional Jew by the fact that she covers her hair. There are more than a few reasons why Orthodox Jewish women cover their hair. Diffidence is the primary reason: when a woman gets married, her hair has a certain sexual effectiveness to it. You'd think that wasn't the case, particularly regarding someone with a bad case of the frizzes (according to Western standards that is). But no, it's true, they believe woman's hair should be saved exclusively for her hubby. A Jewish woman can cover her hair with a hat, a snood or with other things. Wearing a wig is a common practice in the Western world because of the reality that many passionately Orthodox Jewish women are in a work environment and they require dressing the part. Wig hair is either dead or artificial, so it doesn't impact the sexual power that a woman's own natural hair does. This keeps in line with the second motive traditional Jewish woman cover their hair: in order to remain somewhat separate from outside Western culture. When a sacred Jewish woman puts something on her head, it symbolizes that she is one of God's own.

Hair in Native Culture

For most Natives, hair was only cut under certain circumstances. Many Dine, or Navajo, cut the children's hair on their first birthday and then do not cut it again. Among some tribes, hair was cut as part of tribal mourning customs. You can imagine how it must have felt for many Native children to have their hair cut against their will upon entrance into government-run boarding schools.

Despite the European settlers' efforts, the practiced hair customs survived. Thus, Native women tend to have long hair. For many of them, there is meaning in wearing their hair long. That meaning can be found in their tradition, spirituality, identity, personality, and/or individuality. They all have a relationship with their hair. Our hair is a part of who we are. I believe the indigenous people of America truly understand the bigger picture of what hair can do and loving their hair is integrated within their practices.

CHAPTER 4

Understanding the Element

"Knowledge itself is power."
~ Sir Francis Bacon

Understanding Why Hair Grows

*I*t has been documented that anthropologists agree the main purpose of hair on the scalp is to protect us from the sun and other aspects of climate. Your eyelashes, for example, are designed to protect small particles from flying directly into the eyes, as your nose hair protects your nostrils. The sun produces light but it also releases radiation. Hair can filter out some of this radiation but not all of it. Studies show that a full head of hair receives only about 17% of solar radiation.

Now besides these health reasons, did you know your hair can put you in a social class? Within 30 seconds of meeting you, your hair can tell them your social status, age and sometimes even occupation. It is also connected to your sexual being—the flutter of your eyelashes, the slight movement of the neck that allows the hair to glide across your face—all these things are appealing to the opposite sex, no matter what ethnicity you are.

What is the Cuticle?

The cuticle is the outer layer of the hair. It is tightly secured around the hair and it protects the inner cortex and medullae from heat and chemicals. Most African-Americans have a thicker cuticle layer.

What is the Cortex?

The cortex is the middle of the hair, it extends from the hair root and along the hair shaft, the visible section of your hair. The strength of your hair comes from its cortex which also determines both the color and texture of your hair. The cortex is the part of the hair we tamper with when we press, add heat, or put chemicals in our hair. It is the bulk of the hair and is made of keratin. If you don't understand all this just remember that products made with keratin are usually good for our hair.

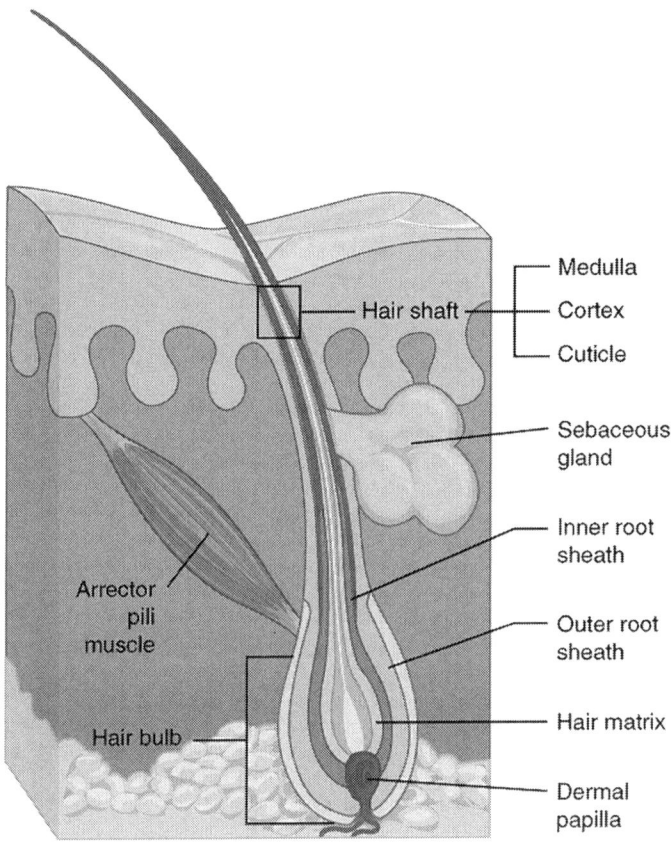

What is Your Hair Type?

ll research brought to us by anthropologists has determined that there are three major ethnic groups of the human race and that each one is associated with a hair type:

1. Negroid – originating in Africa.
2. Caucasoid – originating in Eastern Europe.
3. Mongoloid – originating in Asia.

For the sake of simplicity, I have categorized hair into these types throughout the book so you can find specific information that will work for your type.

1. Negroid – This hair is kinky or has tight curls whether it is thin or thick. This is Type 1 or T1.
2. Caucasoid – This hair is straight. If you are mixed with some Negroid, your hair may have wavier curls or have tight curls with a straight silky texture. It may also be known as --in my opinion-- to those with a slave mentality as "Good Hair." This is Type 2 or T2.
3. Mongoloid – If you are of Asian descent you will find your hair tends to be straight and have thick strand. This is Type 3 or T3.
4. Mixed Race – If you are Negroid with some degree of Caucasoid and/or Mongoloid, your hair may very well fall of the two types T1 or T2, but it will be more of one than the other.

Type Test

Some people have an unrealistic view of their hair type, confused and brainwashed by what is socially accepted as "good hair" or "bad hair". I personally never understood these sayings since I have yet to meet a person whose hair has committed a crime or received an award for being a good member of society. Nevertheless, let's put these into categories.

T1 – Your hair is Type 1 if you are not able to use water alone to lay it flat to your scalp without it lifting and separating back into tiny curls. If you find that your hair curls back to small beautiful curls even slightly and expands and/or thickens when it gets wet, you should follow the instructions T1 outlined throughout the How To's chapter.

T2 – If your hair is able to lay flat to the scalp when wet and/or becomes thin in its natural state meaning, no chemical process other than coloring has been added to your hair, you should follow T2 instructions. If you're still not sure which type you are let me settle this for you. If in doubt consider yourself T1 and the instructions and products will be more likely to work for you.

T3 – This hair type is for men or women of Asian descent. This book will focus on T1 and T2 hair types.

If you are of mixed-race your hair will fit into one of the T1 or T2 categories. Nevertheless, you will find that one hair type is more dominant, so choose that one. Interestingly enough, when I had clients perform the Type Test, many were unhappy with the category their hair fell into and were still in denial as to which instructions they should follow. This led to such a big discussion and that alone was fascinating to me. The important thing to remember is that it is to your benefit to follow the instructions for your true hair type. If you don't, you may hinder your desired results.

"Defeat is not the worst of failures. Not to
have tried is the true failure."
~ Gorge Edward Woodberry

CHAPTER 5

Intentions

*"Not until you understand someone's intentions
do you know if the intent is good or bad"*
~ Desreta Jackson

The BlackSilk Technique

Think about vaccines 20 years ago. You didn't truly understand not all vaccines are good for you. Some vaccines were intended to make you sick so that you would have more medical problems and have to go to the doctors. Thus, making the medical industry even more money. Some can argue that in order to heal you, the vaccines had to make you sick to build your immune system. Both sides of this debate would agree that will for sure be a percentage of individuals that will get sick, and instead of getting better they would be in a worse condition than before taking the vaccine. I ask you this: if their intentions were to make you better, does it make it make the vaccine good? What about if their intentions were to make you sick, does it make the vaccine bad? When you learn the intentions behind the inventor, company, or distributor you then can understand if a product may cause you harm. It would be impossible to know the intentions behind every product on the market but it is not impossible to know if something is working in your favor or not.

When I created the first product for BlackSilk, my intentions were to cure eczema, a skin problem, my 2-year-old daughter had at the time. Since then, every product on the BlackSilk line was created to solve specific problems that have afflicted my friends or loved ones. This is the reason our product line has only specific items listed.

The BlackSilk Technique was created for me to pass down to my daughter that way she will always have a method on how to grow and care for her hair in the event I wasn't around. "The BlackSilk Technique" is designed specifically for African-American hair that is prone to breakage and hard to grow to great lengths. This is not just about how to obtain healthy hair—that part is easy and will come naturally when you start the process. It's maintaining length that's difficult. Each step is vital to the success and longevity of your hair and must be done in sequence and routinely in order to achieve the results you want.

By reading the instructions for each hair type, you will learn "The BlackSilk Technique" and how to use the six-step method which includes my four-step specially formulated products. I will show you the best way to wash, condition and much more according to your hair type and explain the reasons behind the method. In my research, I found that many products on the market that are geared towards African-American hair only give us half the information to grow long, healthy hair and capitalized on a lot of B.S.!

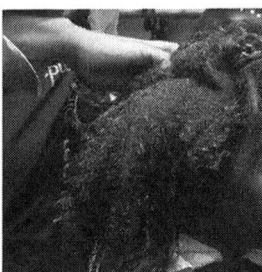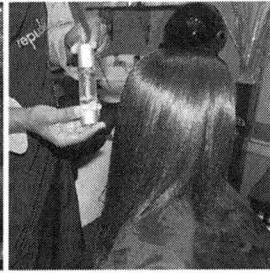

Step by Step

The full system was added to my haircare line under the Silk Hair Growth System. I debated for quite a while whether or not I should include my products in this book. But as the saying goes: Momma ain't raised no fool. How can I not share something I worked so hard on, am so proud of and is something I created based off of my beliefs. This is a step by step how and why to use the Silk Hair Growth System. Please see ordering information in the back of the book.

STEP #1

The Clear Protector

Apply product on slightly damp hair by combing the product throughout the hair in sections. For first time use, ensure the products coats hair from roots to tips. Leave the product on for 30 minutes. For a faster and deeper process, cover hair with a heat cap for 15 minutes. Follow step 2 instructions on how to rinse the product out. Once the product has been used on the whole head, only use this step to retouch your new growth at the roots every 2 months.

The Clear Protector is a remarkable product with a unique safe formula blended to be as close to organic as possible. My strong need for this to be as green as possible is why it has a temporary effect and will need to be used on a regular basis. The longer and more consistent it is used, the stronger the effects will show. Whether you have T1 or T2 hair type, this product is designed to protect the hair from sun damage, breakage, chemical over-processing, and even dryness. You will no longer need a detangling shampoo. It has an instant effect and only takes 10 minutes to apply.

When used on natural hair (virgin hair), it will emphasize the natural curl pattern, add manageability and enhance the natural shine of the hair while protecting and repairing split ends. When used on color-processed hair, it will do all the same things along with protecting the hair color and making the color more vibrant. Most importantly, it will protect hair from the standard damage that surely comes when you color or bleach your hair.

STEP #2

The Silk Conditioning Shampoo

Wash out the Clear Protector with this product by applying shampoo to wet hair, lather, then rinse thoroughly. You may repeat this step if needed.

The Silk Conditioning Shampoo was formulated to be used for all hair types and will rinse out the correct amount of the Clear Protector according to if the hair is virgin or processed. This is very important because it is then setting the correct conditioning power automatically for the next step. Do not expect this product to produce a lot of lather. This product will have a silky feel on the hair while washing and the fragrance will stimulate your senses. You may use this shampoo all over the body, as well as on facial hair to provide silky shiny results on hair and eliminate acne on your body.

STEP #3

The Silk Restoring Conditioner

Apply a generous amount of this product to your hair and scalp. Leave on for 10-20 minutes. For a deep conditioning treatment, cover with a heating cap for 20 minutes then rinse. If a heating cap is not available, cover the hair with a plastic bag and apply a warm damp towel for 20 minutes.

STEP #3A

If wearing your hair natural, leave in the Silk Restoring Conditioner.

STEP #3B

If pressing hair, *lightly* rinse out Silk Restoring Conditioner.

The Silk Restoring Conditioner is loaded with essential proteins needed for our hair and after use will instantly give your hair a soft and smooth feel. You can use this conditioner every day for added softness. It can also be used as a leave-in conditioner or as a hair lotion on natural curls.

STEP #4

Trim your hair (read Trimming Your Hair section for additional details).

STEP #5

After you have done this process in its entirety, I highly recommend protecting your hair from heat and the everyday elements with these two styles that promote great growth for the next two to three months.

Try small to medium individuals or a braided hair weave. I am more than sure that every black woman is more than familiar with this process. If you have a perm you should not do this step until your perm is more than three weeks old. Some of you may even think, "Ha! I can get the same results if I just braid or weave my hair up because it usually gets longer when I do." But, don't forget it always breaks right off and fast, doesn't it? You can braid your hair all day it won't matter; our hair is not strong enough to acquire real length and that is what my products are all about. It will change the way your hair will deal with tension and stress. It will level the playing field for T1 and T2 to gain the strength, elasticity, a protective shield and the missing nutrients needed.

STEP #6

The Sugar and Almond Essence Oil

Apply this product throughout the hair for added shine and nutrients. Use on your scalp to feed your hair. You may use this product after washing your hair, before styling your hair, and/or after styling your hair.

The Sugar and Almond Essence Oil is blended using a pure virgin olive oil base but the key component is a trade secret. This wonderful oil formula is non-greasy or oily and it holds all the nutrients to heal your skin. This product can help relieve muscular aches and pains, reduce eczema and can be used on nails. When taking a bath, add four-six pumps into your water and watch how smooth and moisturize your skin feels. The Sugar and Almond Essence Oil is completely safe for newborn babies.

CHAPTER 6

The Plan

"A goal without a plan is just a wish."
~ Antoine de Saint-Exupéry

The Plan

*L*aying the foundation to gain healthy, long, beautiful hair comes from accepting the hair type and how thick or thin your hair is naturally. The amount of hair strands that you have determines how thick your hair is going to be; as they say, "it is what it is". DNA has predetermined your overall progress; some of you will find your hair grows at a faster rate than others and can reach much greater length than others with very little effort. No matter where you find your hair's condition when you start this process I guarantee you are going to notice a difference in how your hair looks and feels for the better. Doing the BlackSilk Technique will give you the optimum results for *your* hair, not your sister's, your best friend, or that girl you saw three weeks ago. Your hair will become healthier, thicker and much longer. The Plan is to use what your parents gave you and flourish!

Having a realistic goal and making a plan on how to get there will be well worth the effort. My own personal plan started with a calendar and marking off, in advance, the day I would dedicate to doing my hair. I would send the kids off with my mom if I could, and pre-tape my favorite TV shows. Before my "appointment" I would buy my hair extensions if I was going to use them, determine how I was going to style my hair or how I wanted to wear it if pressed. Doing my hair wasn't stressful -- it became more of a "MY DAY" thing. After a few months, I was able to do everything in half the time which only gave me more kickback time!

You should make your own PLAN— maybe not the same way as mine but find something that will work for you, put it on paper and stick to it. It's only once every two months if you're following my Technique, if you can't have a day for yourself that often, trust me, trying to grow beautiful, long hair is the least of your problems!

My Personal Hair Growth

I am so excited and proud to share with you my findings and to debunk *The Hair Conspiracy.* The first step towards truth would be to do the Hair Type Test. Once you know your true hair type, you can read the required chapters on each step. Using the recommended products and the techniques I will share, you can begin the journey to longer, stronger hair.

In the beginning, you may find the process to be tedious, but once done repeatedly -- like anything else -- it will become second nature and a ritual you will respect and love because of the results. I highly recommend only doing the ritual when you have a complete day to devote to it with no rushing or stress. "The BlackSilk Technique" can give you remarkable results whether or not you use a licensed hairdresser who uses the products, practices, or understands the method. You can become your own expert.

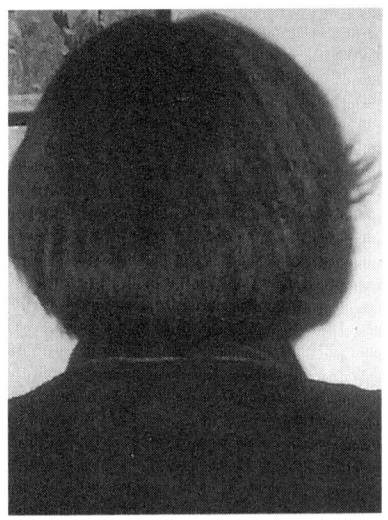

**Notice how dull
my hair looks.**

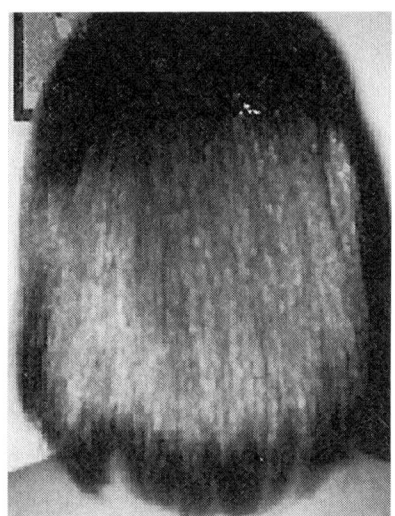

**Three months later
using system.**

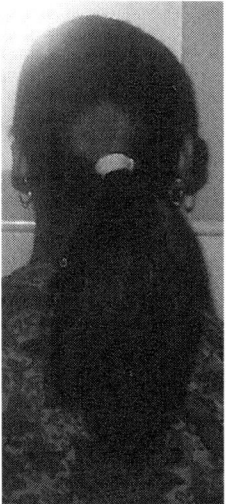

Six more months.

Your Plan and Photo Journal

Start your plan off by getting a calendar and marking off the first day you will dedicate the time to begin the journey to healthier hair. Make notes of what you did to your hair, the products you used, and what you feel works or didn't work out during this process. Along with your monthly notes keeping a photo gallery will help you to stay focused on your goal. You know the saying "out of sight, out of mind"? Well, this will help you to see what is happening to your hair and remind you over time how far you've come. After reading the remaining chapters make a commitment now.

1st Month

Date: _____

Time of Day: _____

Hair Style: _____

1st picture

Give a brief description of the products you used and your ritual.

_____

_____

_____

_____

_____

_____

_____

_____

_____

_____

_____

_____

_____

_____

_____

_____

_____

_____

Hair Notes:

2nd **Month**

Date: _____

Time of Day: _____

Hair Style: _____

Picture

Notes:_____

_____

_____

_____

_____

_____

_____

_____

_____

_____

_____

_____

_____

_____

_____

_____

_____

_____

Hair Notes:

3rd Month

Date: _____

Time of Day: _____

Hair Style: _____

Picture

Notes:_____

_____

_____

_____

_____

_____

_____

_____

_____

_____

_____

_____

_____

_____

_____

_____

_____

_____

Hair Notes:

4th **Month**

Date: _____

Time of Day: _____

Hair Style: _____

2nd picture &
4th month picture

Give a brief description of what you notice works and doesn't work.

_____

_____

_____

_____

_____

_____

_____

_____

_____

_____

_____

_____

_____

_____

Hair Notes:

5th **Month**

Date: _____

Time of Day: _____

Hair Style: _____

Picture

Notes:_____

_____

_____

_____

_____

_____

_____

_____

_____

_____

_____

_____

_____

_____

_____

_____

_____

_____

_____

Hair Notes:

6th **Month**

Date: _____

Time of Day: _____

Hair Style: _____

Picture

Give a brief description of the overall condition of your hair now. By this time, you should have a better understanding of what helps your hair to grow.

_____
_____
_____
_____
_____
_____
_____
_____
_____
_____
_____
_____
_____
_____
_____
_____

Hair Notes:

7th **Month**

Date: _____

Time of Day: _____

Hair Style: _____

Picture

Notes:_____

_____

_____

_____

_____

_____

_____

_____

_____

_____

_____

_____

_____

_____

_____

_____

_____

_____

_____

_____

Hair Notes:

8th Month

Date: _____

Time of Day: _____

Hair Style: _____

Picture

Give a brief description of the products you used and your ritual.

_____
_____
_____
_____
_____
_____
_____
_____
_____
_____
_____
_____
_____
_____
_____
_____

Hair Notes:

9th Month

Date: _____

Time of Day: _____

Hair Style: _____

Picture

Notes:_____

_____

_____

_____

_____

_____

_____

_____

_____

_____

_____

_____

_____

_____

_____

_____

_____

_____

Hair Notes:

10th **Month**

Date: _____

Time of Day: _____

Hair Style: _____

Picture

Give a brief update about your gains and/or losses.

_____

_____

_____

_____

_____

_____

_____

_____

_____

_____

_____

_____

_____

_____

_____

Hair Notes:

11th Month

Date: _____

Time of Day: _____

Hair Style: _____

Picture

Notes:_____

_____

_____

_____

_____

_____

_____

_____

_____

_____

_____

_____

_____

_____

_____

_____

_____

_____

Hair Notes:

12th Month

Date: _____
Time of Day: _____
Hair Style: _____

6th month picture &
12 months picture

Give a brief description of the overall condition of your hair now. By this time, you should have a grand understanding of what helps your hair to grow.

_____
_____
_____
_____
_____
_____
_____
_____
_____
_____
_____
_____
_____
_____

Hair Notes:

CHAPTER 7

Shampooing

"There are no bad shampoos on the market only overly expensive ones that either don't clean well or overly strip your hair of its natural oils."
~ Desreta Jackson

Shampooing

The best way I can say this is: WASH YOUR HAIR! I am so tired of people giving every reason under the sun why they don't like to shampoo their hair. If you have Type 1 hair I believe we are members of a secret society that have all experienced at some point in our lives contemplating shaving all of our hair off or shaving our children's hair off because of how thick it can become when wet! Nevertheless, you still have to wash it! The same way you take a bath so your body feels refreshed and doesn't smell, your hair needs the same thing.

Which shampoo should you use? There are no bad shampoos on the market only overly expensive ones that either don't clean well or overly strip your hair of its natural oils. The best way to find a good shampoo for you is after you've picked the correct conditioner for your hair it will always have a shampoo brand that goes along with it. After a regular shampooing, your hair still retains about 70 to 90 percent of the extractable oils. That's a good thing because otherwise, your hair would be dry and brittle.

When to Shampoo

It is very important that African-Americans do not shampoo their hair every day. Once a week is a great time frame and if your hairstyle allows once every two weeks is even better. As I've expressed before in this chapter, over-washed hair can lead to overly dry hair. Since we already have to battle this beast on a day-to-day basis why make it any harder? If you have T1 or T2 hair, you shouldn't be washing it every day.

> **Tip**: If you sweat a lot and feel you need to wash your hair more often than suggested due to odor there are

organic, waterless shampoos that you can buy that will deodorize and lift some of the dirt and grime from your hair until you are able to give it a standard shampooing. My customers with braids and dreadlocks love this. On the island, we would put a bit of Sea Breeze (a astringent that can cleanse) on a cloth with some water and gently dab the scalp to clean and deodorize it.

How to Shampoo Non-Chemically-Treated Hair

Chemically treated hair if not shampooed correctly, will break and damage easily. Hair that is dyed goes through a special process whose layers of the cortex are stripped and this alone will leave the hair weak. What most people don't know is that when you treat your hair with a chemical it has to apply an extreme amount of heat to the hair shaft in order for it to change. Just like a curling iron your hair is being subject to heat. Hair should be between a pH balance of 0 – 6.9, which is considered an acidic state. A pH balance of 7 is neutral and anything between 7.1 and 14 is alkaline. This natural acidity will stop fungi and bacteria in the hair and head/ scalp. This is when the scalp is considered healthy.

To shampoo your non-chemically treated hair I recommend the following:

1. Wet your hair completely.
2. I recommend then using the BlackSilk shampoo "The Silk Conditioning Shampoo." This is the most vital step that will help to reduce the damage to your hair.
3. Take a small amount into the palm of your hands and massage all over your head. You may notice your hair will not lather at this point if it is not very dirty.
4. Be sure to rinse out the shampoo completely. Repeat steps 2 and 3 of the process, but no more than three times no matter how dirty your hair may be. Washing your hair too many times until it is squeaky clean if you're not a professional, will cause dryness that leads to breaking and unmanageable hair.

How to Shampoo Chemically-Treated Hair

1. Never shampoo your hair with a shampoo that does not say it is for chemically-treated hair. The reason for this is hair that has been chemically-treated has an interrupted pH balance and you need a shampoo that will restore your pH balance. I cannot stress to you how important this step is, except to say that this is one of the leading factors for breakage in chemically-treated hair!
2. Wet your hair completely.
3. For T1, I recommend then using my Clear Protector and comb it through your wet hair using a wide tooth comb. This is the most vital step that will help to reduce the damage to your hair.
4. You may need to use a larger amount of this type of shampoo, the Silk Conditioning Shampoo, to build a good lather.
5. Wait a couple of seconds and allow the lather to work at removing the dirt before you rinse.

Repeat the lathering process no more than twice.

Shampoo and Conditioner in One

Products that contain shampoo and conditioner in one are not a bad idea to use every now and then. However, these types of products should not be used on a regular basis and if you do they should be treated as a shampoo alone for T1 hair. Once you finish washing the hair continue with conditioning instructions for your type of hair. T1 will not benefit from this 2 in 1 process to obtain true length; the only reason you wash your hair is to clean it.

CHAPTER 8

Conditioning

*"Condition: Bring (something) into
the desired state for use."*
~ Oxford Dictionary

Conditioning

The word "conditioning" has two interesting meanings; breaking in is one meaning and taming is the other. These are important aspects we would like to see for our hair, to make it a better condition than what it was. In order to get that out of our hair, we need to do this process every single time we wash our hair.

Did you know using an acid- pH conditioner on the cuticle closes the imbrications? This protects the inner structure of the hair, it also gives shine and luster to the whole surface of the hair. If you get into a good habit of conditioning your hair every time you wash it, it will become stronger and healthier. This process is so important that I believe you should do it even if you haven't washed your hair.

When you condition your hair, you are solving several problems like dullness, dryness, breakage, fly-ways, and most popularly—tangles. If you are trying to acquire length there is no way around this topic. It took me a while when working with the lab to arrive at a great formula for our type of hair.

I am so excited about my Silk Restoring Conditioner. I took the guesswork out of finding the perfect conditioner for T1 and T2 hair types. By sitting under a hairdryer or a heat cap for 15 minutes, you can give yourself a deep conditioning. You may ask how my one conditioner can be great for both T1 and T2 hair types after emphasizing finding the right conditioner for your current hair stage. Well, if you are using the BlackSilk Technique each product from this is designed to work with each other to correct and balance. Therefore, by the time you complete the system with the Protein Conditioner you have now restored your pH balance. No product on the market has been able to do this like how we have done it!

When to Condition

Whenever you wash or wet your hair you should always condition it. I would tell you to think of a conditioner as your best friend. Some will leave you as soon as it gets too difficult, but the great ones have your back no matter how hot of a situation. I created my conditioner to work as a leave-in, deep conditioner if you just use a heating cap or sit under a dryer. You can even lightly rinse part of the conditioner out and press your hair with our conditioner left in. This works great for dry hair. In fact, a great conditioner will allow you to just wash your hair lightly by only using the conditioner with no shampoo, as ours does. This will help for days if you're wearing your hair naturally curly or air drying it and just would like it to become cleaner without shampooing, which can strip some of your natural hair oils. T2 and T3 can wet their hair then put a conditioner in, wait a while, approximately 10 to 20 minutes, rinse it out, then leave it to air dry in its natural form. If you're not going to put heat in your hair this is great on colored hair for optimum sheen and health.

How to Condition

1. On towel dried or slightly damp hair, you should part your hair into two sections using your fingers or a comb.
2. Scoop or pour a generous amount into your hand and finger through one section, then apply another generous amount and do the same to the other section.
3. Then with a wide tooth comb, begin combing it through gently, make sure you comb the ends of your hair first then move to the roots. This will cause less breakage. If you come across any area that is giving you any friction you should apply a little more conditioner to that area.
4. Take a plastic cap and place it over your head (if one is not available you may use a plastic bag). Leave it on your head at least 30 minutes to an hour. I know most conditioners say 1–5 minutes is all it needs but trust me our hair is very thick and to make sure that it penetrates and processes through the entire head of

hair. You will want to do this method each and every time you condition your hair. This technique has been successful for me.

5. Rinse with cool or cold water, this will help to add extra shine to the hair especially if you're trying to blow dry or press afterward. Cold water also helps to close the pores instantly.

How to Pick the Right Conditioner

This part is so simple; yet, it is the hardest thing to do. The beauty industry has bombarded us with so much advertising and products that they have made the possible into the impossible. So, let's try to make this as easy as can be.

If your hair has been colored you need to buy a conditioner that says it is for color treated hair. Now if your hair is permed, buy a conditioner that says it is for permed hair. Let's add a little more to that. What if your hair is colored and it is breaking? Look for a conditioner that says for colored, i.e. chemically treated hair and breaking. Even if you don't see a shampoo for damaged hair but you pick one up for chemically treated hair, chances are your hair will stop breaking anyway because 9 out of 10 times it is breaking because you're using a shampoo and conditioner that is not for chemically treated hair. What if your hair currently isn't colored, permed or processed in any way, then you have what they call normal hair. You haven't done anything that should interrupt your hair's normal process. This means you have free range to select any conditioner that caters to any goal specific need.

> **Tip:** If you're washing your child's or baby's hair, use a shampoo and conditioner made specifically for a child or baby. These products are designed for their delicate hair, skin, and eyes.

Leave–In–Conditioners

I don't recommend this type of conditioner for regular use on T1 hair type. T1 hair needs a deep conditioning every time it is washed to help strengthen it. T2 hair type may use these types of conditioners often since their hair doesn't dry as easily. For a reminder of the different hair types visit Chapter 4.

When Should I Change Conditioners

One week you may find that your hair feels dry and brittle, so you will buy a conditioner that will help it just for that problem. The next month you may not have that problem anymore but you might be worried that your hair doesn't have the body you would like. It is okay to then change to a conditioner that will offer more body. When your hair care needs change, it's okay to change your products; this can even happen weekly.

> **Tip:** You should always use the shampoo that goes with the conditioner, it will usually give you a better overall result.

CHAPTER 9

Offense Defense

"The only defense against the world is a thorough knowledge of it."
~ John Locke

The Clear Protector

I have noticed that when I use to go buy a clear protector at beauty supply stores that target African-American customers there isn't much of a selection to choose from if they have any at all. That's why you can buy this at our website, it is designed to protect your hair from heat, decreasing the damage you otherwise would have received.

Don't worry about what type or name brand to buy just understand these types of products are very much using a lot the same ingredients—you pay mostly for the name brand. Some may have added components to help make your hair feel silky or are designed to use especially when pressing. So, take the time to read the bottle.

Blow Dry

If you can style your hair without using a blow dryer do it! The less heat your hair receives the better, no matter what the type. But if you are going to blow dry there are some things you should know to lessen the damage and add some benefits.

1. Never blow dry your hair unless it's wet or damp.
2. Spritz your hair with a thermal heat protect.
3. Part your hair into four or six large sections.
4. Hold a section of your hair firmly and smoothly comb it from the end of the hair and follow back to the root until you can get one clean pass through with your blow dryer.

T1 and T2 hair should follow the same principles when blow drying.

Tip: Blow dry your hair back to front, it will give you great body and bounce.

Pressing Your Hair

Most people believe that Madam C.J. Walker invented the pressing comb. False. The truth is she made it more popular. The hot comb was developed in Paris at the end of the 1900s. Caucasian women were using it long before to straighten their hair and before that, they used an old-fashioned iron on ironing board if their hair was long enough. Now when Mrs. Walker expanded on this concept and introduced African-American women to a new way of styling our hair she got a bad rap for it. It was said that African-American women who choose to do this method are trying to look white. Even to this day some white Americans still have this belief. I cannot speak for all African-Americans but rest assured when I press my hair I am in no way trying to imitate a Caucasian woman. Instead, I am trying to bring less stress to my life and to get more sleep in the morning because I don't have to wake up an hour earlier to style my hair for work. Besides, until the late 1990s wearing braids or dreadlocks was banned in corporate America. It was considered to be unprofessional and un-groomed.

Here is an interesting fact. The name Dreadlocks derived from the word dreadful. Caucasian Americans disapproved of the natural locking process of some African-Americans so much that they would exclaim, "what dreadful locks." Then over time it was shortened and referred to as Dreadlocks.

Have you ever wondered how much of an influence our perception of our hair has to do with what we have been told vs. our own experience? I have had my Caucasian friends tell me that they can't understand how I could sit through putting my head under such heat that may burn my ear or neck. I jokingly say, "beauty causes pain" but the truth is there is not much of a difference from some of the practices they do for cosmetic reasons either. For example, dyeing their children's hair as young as one-year-old just to look like a natural blond. So instead of judging one another, it is more important to understand and accept.

For those that do press/ flatiron, this type of extensive heat can be very damaging to the hair and I will suggest not doing this method on a regular basis; but, if you do or when the time comes for it the best way to do is the following:

1. Blow dry the hair back to front or upside down.
2. Only press hair that has been freshly washed and conditioned.
3. Before beginning to press your hair make sure it is completely dry. You can test this by placing the blow dryer over your scalp it tends to get if it feels cold your scalp is still wet.
4. Spray the hair with a thermal heat protector.
5. Always test the heating iron for excessive heat using bathroom tissue paper. I like this type of paper because it is very fragile and if you can scorch the tissue paper then you will definitely burn your hair.

   Tip: Never press or retouch your edges without first washing and conditioning your hair. This is the leading cause of breakage.

Hair Greases and Oils

I was very surprised when I found out from my clients who go to hair salons on a regular basis that most of their stylists would complain when they came in with any form of grease or oils on their hair. It just blows me away; I couldn't figure out why they would be so against it. So, I spoke with a couple of friends of mine who are stylists and was shocked by what I learned. It wasn't that they thought this was bad for the hair or that it was an unnecessary step but more so it is a pain in the ass to wash out, especially pomades or beeswax. One said it takes up so much of her shampoo it cuts into her bottom line.

If you are serious about growing your hair to great lengths using the BlackSilk Technique, step 6 requires you to use hair oils or hair grease. To understand this step's significance, you must first understand what hair grease pomades or oils do for our hair, especially if you are a T1. I do recommend using a special blend formula that I've designed to give your hair the true nutrients needed. This is to ensure no guesswork is required on your end.

Our head produces its own natural oils; the straighter your hair is the easier it is for the oil produced from the scalp to flow down to the ends of your hair. The curlier your hair, the more likely your natural oils aren't flowing down very easily to your ends before becoming dry. This is the reason the kinkier your hair is the drier it tends to get. When the hair gets too dry it is more likely to break. But besides all of that, the oil or hair grease we add to our hair helps to work as a shield for our hair shaft against the daily elements of Mother Nature; like cold air and wind which can also lead to dry hair.

I do however discourage the use of heavy pomades in your hair unless it is around the edges/hairline of your scalp. Your hairline is the weakest from being exposed to natural elements. If you use a pomade or pure beeswax on this area you will find it will not break as easily.

We Struck Oil

If you're wearing braids I recommend oiling or greasing your entire scalp and braids twice a week. You will find when it is time to take them down your hair will feel softer and you will have less breakage. For African-Americans with T1 type of hair, it is always good practices to use oil on your hair once a week for the reasons recommended. I personally have a homemade Special Blend that I always recommend to my clients who want to grow their hair or are seeking healthier hair. What makes this blend so unique is it contains a special protein designed to feed the hair. I do offer this on the website.

A person with T2 hair type doesn't usually have the same need for oils or grease so you should use it very sparingly.

CHAPTER 10

Sulfate-Free vs. Sulfate

*"If you make peace without defense power,
then you should be really ready to be ruled."*
- Toba Beta

Sulfate- free vs. Sulfate

*W*hen a product claims to be "sulfate-free", it's typically free of one of three commonly used compounds in shampoos: Sodium Laureth Sulfate, Ammonium Laureth Sulfate or Sodium Lauryl Sulfate. These are also called compounds known as SLES, ALS, and SLS. These chemicals are a mixture of molecules that attract water and oil, and it contains a unique property that allows soaps to separate dirt and oil from things like your skin and hair. This is very important since it is purpose of shampooing or washing! Without these ingredients in cleaning products, they won't clean very well. Now if they are used too often or if there is a high dosage amount of sulfate then it can lead to stripping the body or hair of its natural oils. That is why I recommend for a person whose hair type requires for them to wash their hair every day or hair twice a day, due to excessive oily build up, activities like swimming, or intense sports to use sulfate-free or low sulfate shampoos to help not strip or damage the skin or hair.

The fact of the matter is sulfate–free shampoos can strip your hair as well. Yes, you read it correctly, a sulfate-free shampoo can also strip your hair; if you don't want any of your natural oils stripped away the only thing you can do is not wash your hair. Sulfates are used in many personal care products because they are very effective, and in a fighting match side by side, they are the most effective shampoos for cleaning all hair types and that has been proven from science.

Another false claim is that sulfates strip your hair color. There is no data that proves this. In fact, more scientists are now relating it to the harsh water and the metal contents found in our drinking water.

I just would like for us to become more of a nation that inquires and understands why some things are being used vs. why others are not. Once we get to the root of the information we will understand that everyone and everything is biased. However, being biased is not the problem if you both have the same agenda! Understanding why you want to be sulfate-free is key. Understanding what they consider to be sulfate-free is even more important.

Cradle Cap

If you have ever been around newborns or very small children you've likely heard of cradle cap. It comes from the baby's body oils and old skin that builds up on the head, forehead or eyebrows. You may notice it as a yellow oily crust or scales. Wash baby's head with a baby shampoo to get rid of cradle cap. It is very important as discussed in the earlier chapters to use the right shampoo.

1. While the shampoo is on the baby's head, brush head with a soft baby brush. It will help lift the crust up.
2. Using a fine-tooth baby comb, comb away scales.
3. Then rinse the baby's head well.
4. If there is still more crust wet the head again with more shampoo, let sit for 1-2 minutes and repeat.
5. Some hair may come out but it will grow back.

More importantly, if cradle cap does not go away after two weeks of washing and brushing or if you notice a watery rash behind the ears call your doctor.

Dandruff

---

*A*t one point everyone has some form of dandruff; but, for those who really struggle with it know it is not unsolvable. The trick is to buy two or three medicated shampoos that you will rotate in between shampoos. The reason for this is because at some point that medicated shampoo will lose its effectiveness. Dandruff may be the result of a dry scalp, or a skin condition called seborrheic dermatitis. It could also be caused by eczema, or psoriasis, or an overgrowth of a yeast-like substance (pityrosporum ovale). It can cause itchy scalp and fine white scales. You can even get it on your eyebrows. But there's good news and bad news, the good news is it can be controlled. The bad news is there is no cure. But trust me, to everyone else around you it's not that big of a deal. In all my years, I have never heard of a man who said, "Ay man, I'm not going to get with her because she has dandruff." Also, if you're a black woman who has ever complained that you refuse to date a man with dandruff—you're stupid.

How to Treat Dandruff

A standard medicated shampoo will cure your problems, my two favorites are Head and Shoulders and Neutrogena Healthy Scalp Anti-Dandruff shampoo (the latter has since been discontinued). I like those because they worked and they had been around a long time. People with a constant dandruff problem need to wash their hair twice a week and then you will notice the problem is more under control.

How to Shampoo Dandruff

1. Apply a generous amount of baby oil to your scalp.
2. Then with a comb or brush vigorously comb or brush your scalp until the flakes are lifted from your scalp.
3. Then wet your scalp immensely.
4. Pour a generous amount of the medicated shampoo of your choice into the palms of your hands and massage it all over your scalp.
5. Then as you rinse it out of your scalp try to gently comb or brush again.
6. Repeat this process a few times before conditioning your hair.

If you find that you have a more severe case of dandruff I would recommend you see your doctor, it can be treated with a pill called Nizoral and even with certain creams.

I had this client/friend who had a severe case of dandruff around her forehead. It resembled cradle cap like in a newborn baby. Every time she would remove it, it left a two-tone ring around her head. It bothered her immensely and she would ask me over and over what could she do for it. Every time I gave her advice it would go in one ear and out the other. See, she was the type who only wanted to hear what she wanted to hear. A year later she called me again and asked me once again what can she do about it? She said, "I've tried everything and nothing works." I then said to her, "Did you really try everything or did you try what you wanted?" Sometimes we still have problems not because we weren't given good advice and told how to handle it but because we still want to handle it our way. But if your way was working you wouldn't have had to ask for help in the first place.

> **Home Remedy Tip:** Aspirin will do wonders, it contains the same active ingredient (salicylic acid) as many medicated dandruff shampoos. Keep flaking in check by crushing two aspirins to a fine powder and adding it to the normal amount of shampoo you use each time you wash your hair. Leave the mixture on your hair for 1-2 minutes, then rinse well and wash again with plain shampoo.

Ringworm of the Scalp

R ingworm, also called Tinea Corporis, occurs on the surface of the skin. Ringworm of the scalp is an infection of the scalp caused by many types of fungus, similar to those that cause athlete's foot. It affects children. It is contagious, spreading rapidly from child to child. You may notice a small circle of bumps on the scalp. You should immediately cover with a band-aid and see a doctor. You can decrease the spreading by constantly washing your hands and the infected scalp.

Ringworm causes a scaly, crusted rash that may appear as round, red patches on the skin. Other symptoms and signs of ringworm include patches of hair loss or scaling on the scalp, itching, and blister-like lesions.

Ringworm is contagious and can be passed from person to person by contact with infected skin areas or by sharing combs and brushes, other personal care items, or clothing. It is also possible to become infected with ringworm after coming in contact with a locker room or pool surfaces. The infection can also affect dogs and cats, and pets may transmit the infection to humans. It is common to have several areas of ringworm at once in different body areas.

Treatment

Your doctor will more than likely give you a cream to place on the infected area but for more severe cases you will get something internally. You will need antifungal medications from a doctor to be used either topically or orally.

> **Home Remedy Tip:** Scrub the infected area three times
> a day with a fresh slice of lemon or lime and let it sit and

air dry for approximately two weeks or until it is visually cleared up. If your case is more severe, this method may not work and you will need to see a doctor.

Traction Alopecia

*T*raction Alopecia is the loss of hair generally along the hairline. It's typically caused when the hair has been braided so tight, especially at the sides near the ears at the nape of the neck and around the hairline. It can also be a result of hairstyles that involves tight ponytails or wig glue. It kills me when I see this, especially in women who perm their hair. We all know that friend of the family who is missing their hairline and they just keep wearing those tight braids or ponytails and the braids start moving further and further away from their hairline. And it's like everyone else can see your braids are too tight but you! I know braiders that are so heavy-handed, clients have said to them it feels like my head is bleeding. You can stop going bald by stop pulling your hair out of your scalp!

How to Treat Traction Alopecia

I have been braiding for 20 years and I have found when a braider braids that tightly, they are inexperienced, and it is that insecurity of what they are doing that causes them to braid your scalp and not the hair.

> **Tip:** Look at the braider's own hair, if she or he is going bald don't let them braid your hair. If you have the opportunity look at their own children's hair and if they have traction alopecia, then that is not a good braider.

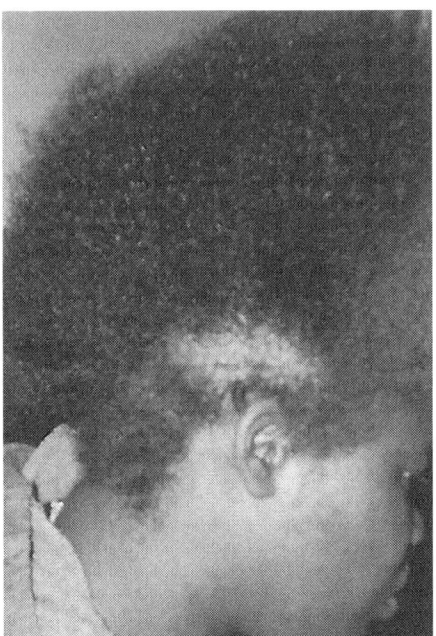

This was the result of constantly putting
her hair in tight ponytails.

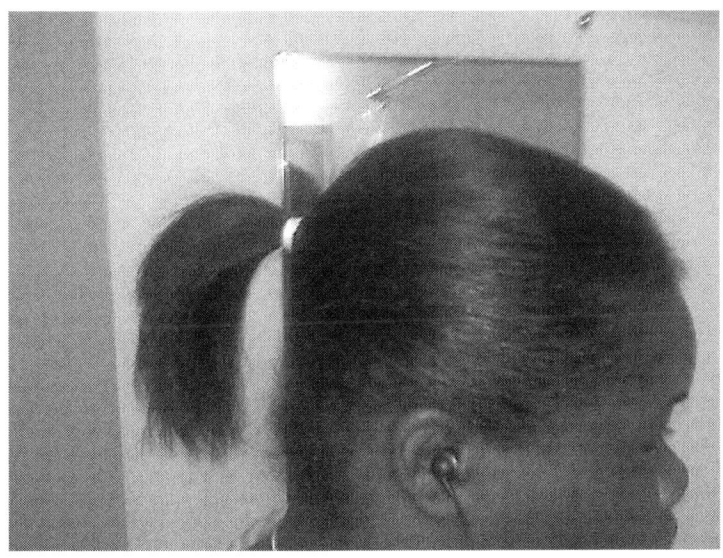

This recovery was the result of a BlackSilk's
Vegetarian Hair, Skin, and Nails Vitamins
& The BlackSilk Technique.

CHAPTER 11

The Truth About Vitamins

*"Truth is everybody is going to hurt you: you
just gotta find the ones worth suffering for."*
~ Bob Marley

The Truth About Vitamins

I always knew vitamins are important for a healthy body but even I had an enlightening experience that proved to me it is a key part for healthy long hair. During the 12 years of perfecting the BlackSilk Technique, I had a friend who was interested in being a part of a hair growing study I was conducting. Like all my clients we would keep detailed records of all treatments and appointments. She was an excellent client never allowing anyone to touch her hair and making sure she would follow all of my advice. Well, a year and a half went by and her hair had only grown three inches more. It would frustrate me because I had cancer patients who were only off treatment for about six months who were getting more hair growth than her.

Then one day she offered to help me out for the day in my office. I noticed that within a sixteen-hour work day she had only eaten twice. A soft taco from Jack-In-The-Box around noon that day and two chocolate chip cookies 30 minutes before we were closing up. Now she is a very thin girl but I never thought much about it. I then had an idea to introduce vitamins into her regimen. Within less than six months her hair showed more growth than the whole year and a half.

Most people take in an adequate number of calories and nutrients but for those rare cases where you're not eating healthy enough or on a vigorous diet, I do suggest vitamins.

Not Required by Law

The reason I call this section, "Not Required by Law" is because our nation's fast food restaurants and other eating establishments are not legally obligated to serve nutritious foods. As a result, our bodies are lacking so many nutrients, and how could you not believe it is affecting your hair?

Vitamin F is found in your fatty acids. You will get more than enough from cooking with oils and from fish products. This vitamin plays a big role in hair and regeneration. Iron is also very important, especially if you have an iron deficiency; you should be taking iron pills anyway and your doctor would require this if you are anemic. Iron deficiency leads to brittle hair. Vitamin B-1, B-2, and B-6 directly affect your hair. A lack of B vitamins has been documented to cause dullness and dandruff problems. While vitamin C helps to bring blood to your follicles. I could go on and on as to how they can help your hair but most of you won't read on anyway and for the ones that would read on you're the few who will apply it to your regimen, so here is the point: get a multivitamin and take it regularly. It's good for your body and hair.

The Shield

Let's talk about iron or the Shield as I call it. An iron deficiency isn't the main reason for unhealthy hair but it can lead to the breaking of your hair, low energy and an overall feeling of weakness. There are some tests that your doctor can give you to determine if you this deficit. Over time the name of the test may change, so you should ask your doctor for a test to see if you're anemic. Besides helping with the overall improvement of your hair it is also great for your nails. Even if you don't think you have an iron deficiency, incorporating vitamins into your diet will only improve your overall health.

> **Home Remedy Tip:** Squeeze lemon juice in your water, it will cause the water to become more alkaline and when you drink it your body will produce a lot of minerals, the kind you need for strong hair.

CHAPTER 12

How To Care For Her

"Not until you are willing to lose will you truly win"
~ Desreta Jackson

Trimming Your Hair

*A*s I clear my throat, firmly rise my head and deepen my voice: to my fellow Americans, my fellow African-Americans, it's hair. It will grow back.

A split end does not help your hair to look thicker because it has now split into two thin, weak strands instead of one. Now I'm not going to say all of us but on average a lot of us aren't very happy with the word trim. And we give our hairdresser a really hard time about the difference between cutting and trimming our hair. I personally don't believe they get a fair rap for this. See it from their point of view for a minute. You sit down in their chair and they have to look at these horrible raggedy ends that haven't been trimmed in God knows how long. Quite often the hair is so damaged it is just a matter of time before the hair starts to break off. But then you're going to complain that they are the ones breaking your hair off. Most people I know hate to have a beautician trim their hair. If you ask a sister when was the last time she trimmed her hair she would likely shift her eyes towards her forehead and after several seconds say something like three years ago or if she's a snappy liar "A year ago." Generally, I can look at someone's hair and determine if they have had a good trim within the last couple of months. If you are following the BlackSilk Technique your ends should get trimmed every four months. Since I suggest braiding or weaving your hair up as part of the technique for no longer than two months; that means every other session when you are doing each step in the BlackSilk Technique one of them should include a trim. I always say sometimes the only way to move forward is by removing just a little bit of the past that no longer provides us with a healthy future.

How to Prevent a Big Mistake

A split end is when one hair strand splits at the end of that strand into two or more strands. Due to the process of splitting the hair becomes even weaker and breaks very easily. What most people don't understand is that sometimes it can keep splitting up the hair shaft. With split ends, there is no way you can accumulate any real length. And your hairdresser knows this, which why they are always trimming your hair.

Understand that anything you use that says it will repair the split end is only temporary. I do advocate using these types of products but there's an old saying I stand by; an ounce of prevention is better than a pound of cure. You should have your hair trimmed regularly if you use chemicals or regularly press your hair. It should be at least once every three mounts. If your hair is kept braided or weaved on a regular basis then twice a year is sufficient. But just remember that if you do not go consistently, your initial trim may be more of a cut.

The Stalemate

The stalemate is a term I use when you find that your hair length has been at a certain length for a really, really long time. For some of you who already have a pretty nice length, but it has never really gotten much longer your hair is at a stalemate and the only way to get out of this bad cycle is to do a major cut and follow my Mahoganize Technique to the "T".

Hold up your index finger and you will notice that it is divided into three with dark lines. Measure one and a half sections then cut that much off of your hair no matter what the length of your hair is to start. If you're at a stalemate you're going to have to cut off the bad ends and it usually goes far up the hair strands. If your hair is not long enough to cut that much off, you should cut at least one half of the length you currently have and then start the steps. I have found that part of the problem with the stalemate is we tend to repeat the same steps and behavior that is causing our problems, so even if we do trim our hair we are neglecting a much deeper problem that can hinder us from progressing. If you cut your hair without following the steps you are more likely to only repeat the problem, for just like in life a fresh start is only as good as the actions that follow.

There will be some of you who will pick and choose which instructions you will follow and which ones you can get away with not applying for various reasons. I am also sure you practice this all the time in other areas of your life and then you later complain. For those of you who fall into this category I can only lead you to water, it's up to you to drink, not sip!

> **TIP:** Trimming split ends is more of a skilled technique. So, have a professional do it on a regular basis because you can stunt your growth by trimming too frequently and trimming too much but if you don't trim off enough of the bad ends it is like you didn't trim at all.

CHAPTER 13

The Perceptions of Braids and Weaves

*"No one can make you feel inferior
without your consent."*
~ Eleanor Roosevelt

Braids and Weaves

*D*uring the time I was doing reach for the book I found out some of the most interesting things about the perceptions that other cultures have of African-Americans. At first, I was livid with my findings but now I have more understanding of the ignorance. An example of one of these misunderstand perceptions is that we wear our hair weaves in an attempt to look white. Another perception is when any other nationality besides Anglo-Saxons wears colored contacts it is perceived as trying to look white. But if a Caucasian person wears colored contacts they're just having fun with changing their eye color. If they wear hair extensions it's for various reasons like for fullness, convenience, a change, etc. However, when African-Americans wear hair extensions we are not embracing our heritage. As I have said before I cannot speak for all African-Americans but let me speak for myself.

I am a dark-complexioned young woman who wears color contacts. I also enjoy manipulating my hair in many styles ranging from weaves to braids to my natural hair at times. But never once have I ever put in contacts or sewed in a weave and thought "this is going to help me look whiter" nor do I believe that when I put acrylic nails on that I am fooling anyone into believing my nails are perfectly shaped, thick and long. I wear contacts because they feel sexier to me than glasses. I wear colored ones sometimes because I get bored with the plain ones. Our type is so versatile it allows me the range to wear it how please. Often times I wear my hair in protective styles but I also change things up for a variety of reasons. I wear weaves sometimes because I might want longer or shorter hair that month or a change in my appearance. Braids are less of a hassle than getting my hair pressed every week, plus I can have sex more often with my husband because I don't sweat it out. I could go on and on because my reason could change due to the occasion.

In the search to understand how we can achieve longer, healthier hair I have found that it is essential for us to have this variety of change in our hair. It gives the hair a period of rest that will allow you to accumulate growth. I recommend finding a great braider or weaver because the wrong one will take years of growth away in one second with bad habits or techniques.

Signs of a Bad Braider

1. Ask to see pictures of their work, if she/he cannot provide an album worth of pictures there is a reason.
2. Look at the starting points of the braid. If there is a lot of tension don't negotiate with the braider, they can't change years of bad habits overnight. Continue looking for someone else because this will pull your edges out resulting in Traction Alopecia.
3. Their prices are way below the current market for the same service. There is some truth to "you get what you pay for", so if the braider thought she was worth more she would be asking for it.

How to Take Care of Your Braids

1. You should wash and condition your braids once every 30 days your braids are worn for T1 hair type and twice every 30 days for T2 type. If dandruff is not a problem for you, you don't sweat much, or if you aren't doing any swimming during this time there is nothing wrong with T1 hair not being washed until you take the braids down if you have had them in for less than 60 days.
2. Apply a scalp grease or hair oil once a week. This will help to prevent drying and protect the hair by coating it.
3. When you are taking your braids out never take them out dry. Use a spray bottle filled with a mixture of 90% water and 10 % conditioner. Saturate your hair from root to end before the takedown process.

Notice no tension/ pulling on the edges. Notice the pulling at the beginning of the braid.

There shouldn't be signs of any tension at the base of the hair as if it is pulling.

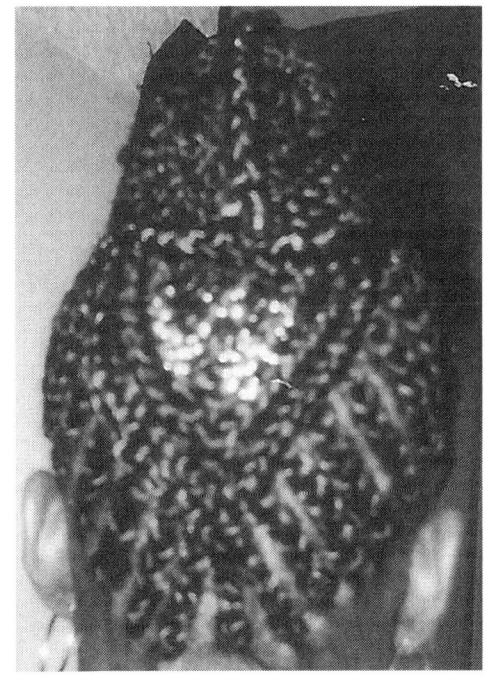

Signs of a Good Weaver

1. Ask to see pictures of their work, they should have a variety of clients and styles to fill an album worth of pictures.
2. Most good weavers wear their product and wear it well. Check out the stylist's hair, if you like their look you're probably going to like her work too.
3. Look at pictures of how she braids the base of the weave. Just like anything else in life, a good foundation is vital. It should look small and neat. Some weavers really don't know how to put on a good weave but because they are hair stylists. They know how to style it afterward making it look great, but the foundation is just as important. Your weave won't last long without a good foundation. Also, remember the foundation is your hair and a bad weaver can damage this each and every time they braid or pack it away!
4. Once the weave has been applied to your hair any residual pain should go away on its own, within an hour or two. Anything other than that is a sign the hair has been braided or sewed too tightly and the tension will only be relieved by the hair breaking.

How to Take Care of Your Hair Weave

1. It is very important to still wash and condition your own hair along with your extensions. I suggest using a leave-in-conditioner during this time. It works well because you can squirt it in-between the braids and rub it through with your hands and move on to drying/styling your weave.
2. If you are wearing a curly weave, a great way to keep it soft and healthy looking is to use a conditioner on the hair right after you wet it. The more conditioner you use will help it to keep its curly form. An expensive conditioner is not needed; I personally like the fruity kind for the scented experience.
3. Never wear your weave for longer than 60 days. T1 hair type tends to start matting very quickly and you will find that you start to lose more hair when it is time to take down the weave.

4. Try to wear a style that braids your entire hair up because usually the part that's braided is what will grow, so if you cannot braid it all in try to vary things up with styles that leave out different sections of your own hair. This way you're giving parts of you're a chance to rest and grow.

5. It is very important to oil your own hair during this time. I have a Special Blend of nutrients and oils that I would use exclusively on my clients.

Combs and Brushes

*I*n the 1800s there was a belief that if you brush your hair 100 strokes before bed it made your hair healthier. Well, in the 1800s it would appear that this was a good idea. It was meant for those times and directed for the European women and men. During those times people didn't take baths every day or wash their hair often. Thus, their hair would accumulate a buildup of dust, oil, and dirt. By brushing the hair 100 times it would brush away some of that build up leaving the hair much shinier and healthier looking.

T1 hair type should avoid brushing altogether. This hair type is very weak and doesn't lend itself to the pulling and friction of a brush. T2 hair type can tolerate this much better due to the fact that it is stronger and not as kinky. However, brushing should be limited and a round-tip brush should be used if either type desires to brush.

How to Brush

1. Try not to brush your hair excessively when it's wet. Because all hair types are weaker when wet, and more fragile.
2. T1 hair shouldn't use any brushes with shaped or close-spaced teeth. If you choose to brush, spray a little oil sheen on the brush, it will reduce the friction and result in less breakage.
3. The wider-tooth brushes with round ends are best to use, or a comb with small teeth.

How to Comb

1. You should have three types of combs. A wide-tooth comb for your everyday combing and detangling. A rattail comb for parting the hair for hairstyles. A fine-tooth comb is great for pulling your hair strands together to create a brushing effect.
2. You should comb your hair in small sections. Hold the section at the base firmly and gently comb the ends out then moving to the base of your hair. After smoothly combing from the ends to the base, make a pass combing from your scalp to ends.
3. When your hair is wet, only use a detangling comb. These are generally very large combs with wide spaces in between each tooth of the comb.
4. Always use a detangling spray when combing your hair after washing.

CHAPTER 14

Good Hair VS. Bad Hair

*"The most rediouly phase I have ever heard.
As if someones hair robbed a bank and did a
crime therefore it was labeled bad hair"*
- Desreta Jackson

Good Hair vs. Bad Hair

This subject along with the light and dark-skinned issues is one of the saddest, most ignorant displays of the crippling effects that slavery has done to us. It used to infuriate me when I heard someone stress or highlight their hair type or skin color as a selling point to their self-worth. That is until I realized how insignificant they must feel their life accomplishments are. It is very rare you'll hear someone say, "I have my Ph.D. now and I'm light skinned too" or "I have invented a revolutionary product and I have good hair too." But far too often you'll hear a young lady or man discuss their best attributes and it would sound something like this: "I'm 24 years old, light skin, long hair and I have a big ass." They say it as if these were accomplishments or characteristics of their personality.

I can personally tell you that this issue never became ubiquitous in my own home until something happened with one my closest friends, a person whom I have spent time discussing the works of Beethoven, the history of Malcolm X, the Black Panthers, the thinking of Dr. King and the beginning of the Egyptians. Only to have him say to me one day that he believes the reason some lighter skinned people get darker is because they are around darker skinned people excessively. I would have excused his thinking if he smoked weed or drank a lot. But he does not. This friend is mixed race and his own mother is a darker skinned woman. I knew then that Francis Galton's theory of Nature vs. Nurture goes deeper than I really thought. As intelligent as this man and his family was; it was no match for the lessons portrayed in his environment.

I began to realize the Willie Lynch Speech did exactly what it said it would do and instead of enslaving our minds for 300 years it has permanently programmed us with a way of thinking that we may never overcome. Maybe the answer is not to try to forget the past mindsets, for it will never truly erase. Like a computer that has been previously filled with information, even after it has been deleted it is still showing signs of previous use and depending on the level of knowledge of the person trying to recover the lost information it can always be restored to some degree. Therefore, I believe we need to replace that slave mentality with new and correct information. By passing this down to the newer generations over time the beliefs and thinking will change for the better.

For those of you who are not familiar with the notorious Willie Lynch, he was considered an expert at seasoning black slaves. He was so well known for his success that it was said he was sought out by slave owners to teach them his technique. Upon going to Virginia in 1712, he supposedly delivered a very controversial speech about controlling slaves. The speech was circulated under the title, "Willie Lynch Letter: The Making of a Slave." Even though the letter was later determined to be false, I still found it very powerful and would like to share.

CHAPTER 15

The Willie Lynch Letter

"My Plan is guaranteed and the good thing about this is that if used intensely for one year the slaves themselves will remain perpetually distrustful."
~ Willie Lynch (Unknown)

The Willie Lynch Letter

Gentlemen:

I greet you here on the bank of the James River in the year of our Lord, one thousand seven hundred and twelve. First, I shall thank you the men of the Colony of Virginia for bringing me here. I am here to help you solve some of your problems with the slaves. Your invitation reached me on my modest plantation in the West Indies where I have experimented with some of the newest and still the oldest program is implemented. As our boat sailed south of the James River, I saw enough to know that your problem is not unique. While Rome used cords of wood as crosses for standing human bodies along its highways in great numbers, you are here using the tree and rope on occasion.

I caught the whiff of a dead slave hanging from a tree a couple of miles back. You are not only losing valuable stock by hangings, you are having uprisings; slaves are running away, your crops are sometimes left in the field too long for maximum profit. You suffer occasional fires, your animals are killed. Gentlemen, you know what your problems are; I do not need to elaborate. I am not here to enumerate your problems. I am here to introduce you to a method of solving them.

In my bag here, I have a fool-proof method for controlling your black slaves. I guarantee every one of you that if installed correctly it will control the slaves for at least 300 years. My method is simple and members of your family and any overseer can use it.

I have outlined a number of differences among the slaves; and I take these differences and make them bigger. I use fear, distrust, and envy for control purposes. These methods have worked on my modest plantation in the West Indies and it will work throughout the South. Take this simple little list of differences, think about them. On top of my list is "age", but it is there only because it starts with an "a," the second is "color" (shade), there is intelligence, size, sex, size of plantation, status on plantation, attitude of owner, whether the slaves live in the valley, on the hill, east, west, north, south, have fine hair or coarse hair, or is tall or short. Now that you have a list of differences, that distrust is stronger than trust, and envy is stronger than adulation, respect or admiration.

The black slaves after receiving this indoctrination shall carry on and will become self-refueling and self-generating for hundreds of years, maybe thousands; don't forget you must pitch the old black vs. the young black male and the young black male vs. the old black male. You must use the dark skin slaves vs. the light skin slaves and the light skin slaves vs. the dark skin slaves. You must also have your white servants and overseers distrust ALL blacks, but it is necessary they trust and depend on us. They must love, respect, and trust ONLY us.

Gentlemen, these kits are your control; use them. Have your wives and children use them, never miss an opportunity. My plan is guaranteed and the good thing about this plan is that if used intensely for one year the slaves themselves will remain perpetually distrustful.

Thank you, gentlemen,
Willie Lynch, 1712
Unknown original source
Printed 1997 Claud Anderson Dirty Little Secrets

CHAPTER 16

Lies Mama Told

"Don't Believe the Hype"
~ Public Enemy

The Top Five Myths Revealed

*Y*ou will continue to be fooled by the mainstream market of bad hair products and snake oils design to take your money. Your hair is the first line of defense and source of your energy and powers and if someone can convince you to cover it, destroy it, or be ashamed of it! The battle is half won.

MYTH #1

Dirt grows your hair.

ANSWER

True

REASON

The saying "dirt grows your hair" originated from people noticing that when they didn't wash their hair very often it didn't break as much leading to their hair to grow longer. It wasn't actually the dirt that was helping it to become longer but the fact that in order for their hair to become dirty or smelly it went some time without washing. When it comes to very curly or kinky hair it takes a while for the hair's natural oils to reach all the coils of the hair. By allowing the hair to build upon natural oils along with adding it, you will retain more moisture which will help the hair to become stronger and have more elasticity to bounce back from the day to day wear of the natural elements. So, yes, they were right because washing your hair too much can lead to dry hair, resulting in weak and brittle hair stands if you wash the hair too frequently—therefore, a little dirt doesn't hurt.

MYTH #2

African-American hair is the strongest hair there is.

ANSWER

False

REASON

In fact, T1 hair type is one of the weakest hair types there is. If you were to pluck out a strand of an African-American's hair and place it next to other hair types, you would see that the density of our hair is much thinner. If you would think of it like a piece of thread, the thinner the thread is the easier it is for you to snap it. This is the leading factor as to why we have a hard time accumulating length. It has been studied that Asian hair is the thickest hair strand, which is the reason it is one of the hardest to color and curl.

MYTH #3

Washing your hair with an egg strengthens it.

ANSWER

False

REASON

The egg on hair concept was used as a conditioner and not a shampooing method. The concept was that the protein from the egg was supposed to be the strengthening factor, but the type of protein in an egg is actually too large to penetrate the hair shaft enough to do any real good as a conditioner. However, egg whites used with your shampoo are good for thin hair because the protein will coat the hair and help it to appear fuller.

MYTH #4

Braids are bad for your hair.

ANSWER

False

REASON

Braids aren't bad for the hair but there are bad braiders. T1 hair type can benefit from this process tremendously. It allows the hair to rest from the pulling that naturally comes from combing and brushing. It also gives the hair a rest from elements such as the wind and heat that can promote more drying of the hair, leading to brittle hair and split ends. A bad braider can put too much tension on the hair follicles or hair strands that will eventually lead to snapping or breaking either from the root or the hair strand itself.

MYTH #5

Using peppers on your hair or scalp will help it to grow.

ANSWER

False

REASON

The burning stimulation on the scalp can help to increase blood flow and blood flow to the scalp is essential to receiving oxygen needed for your hair cells to promote hair growth, but this will not help your hair to grow. I don't recommend this since no research has been done to show the effects on the skin irritation and the long-term effects resulting from the burning and for the added damages this may do to the scalp. Increase in blood flow can easily be obtained by a head massage, vigorously brushing or even standing upside down on your head can stimulate the same amount of blood flow so why use peppers? Let there be no misunderstanding, the average person's head produces more than enough flow of blood to the scalp and needs no added help. If you're going bald or having major hair loss, you should see a doctor.

Home Remedy Tips

Dandruff:

1. Skip the shampoo and go right to rinsing. Try wetting your hair and rubbing some **baking soda** vigorously into your scalp, let it sit for 10 minutes then wash out with your shampoo and conditioner. Baking soda reduces overactive fungi that can cause dandruff. Your hair may get dried out at first, but then after a few weeks, your scalp will start producing natural oils, leaving your hair softer and free of flakes.
2. Just mix 2 tablespoons **lemon juice** into your scalp and rinse with water. Then stir 1 teaspoon lemon juice into 1 cup water and rinse your hair with it. Repeat this once daily until your dandruff disappears. It will help acidity and balance the pH of your scalp, which helps keeps dandruff away.
3. Take Vitamin B. It has been documented that the lack of taking B-complex vitamins is associated with dandruff.

Dry Hair:

1. **Bananas**. Back home on the island sometimes we would use bananas as a natural remedy for the treatment of dry hair. They are rich in potassium, antioxidants, and vitamins. For the treatment of dry hair, you need to make a banana paste. Just blend two overly ripe bananas and add one tablespoon each of coconut oil, honey, and olive oil. Apply this paste on hair for 15 minutes. Wash off your hair with warm water.

2. You can also use **bananas with egg**. Grind two overly ripe bananas and add 2 eggs. Beat the mixture properly adding a few drops of honey to it. Apply this pack on hair and scalp. After half an hour, rinse off with shampoo.

3. **Olive Oil** is the best treatment for dry hair. Olive oil can be used for massaging your head or as a hair pack. All you need to do is to warm some olive oil. Apply it on the scalp with your fingertips. Massage your hair for some time. Rinse your hair with a shampoo to remove oil from hair. To prepare olive oil pack, you are required to blend one egg and a peeled cucumber. Add four tablespoons of olive oil to it. Apply the mixture on hair and wear a shower cap on head, leave on for about 15 minutes, and then wash off your hair twice with a pH balanced shampoo like the BlackSilk Conditioning Shampoo.

4. **Water.** It is as simple as just adding water to your hair. When you're thirsty, what do you do to quench the thirst? Add water.

Split Ends:

1. 1 **avocado**, pitted and skinned, 2 tablespoons **egg whites** and 3 tablespoons **olive oil**. Mash up the avocado and mix in the egg whites and olive oil. Whip until you obtain a creamy consistency like conditioner. Apply to your hair, cover with a shower cap and let sit for 45 minutes to an hour. Rinse thoroughly and wash hair with a mild, natural shampoo to get the mixture out but let the nutrients keep working. This is just a temporary remedy to help keep the hair from splitting.

CHAPTER 17

Your Hair's Connection to The Universe

"Meditation brings wisdom; lack of meditation leaves ignorance. Know well what leads you forward and what holds you back and choose the path that leads to wisdom."
~ Buddha

Your Hair's Connection to the Universe

*Q*uantum Physics has many ways to prove to you that your hair is connected to the universe in many ways. One of the latest discoveries about hair concerns melanin, the pigment in hair. An 18-year-old in Nepal recently discovered, that the melanin in your hair is light sensitive and can be used as a conductor. He has now been using human hair to replace silicon in solar panels. This is an extraordinary find especially in poorer countries the price of hair is dramatically cheaper than silicon. Plus, you can personally grow and control your own inventory allowing you to bring down the cost of solar panels and give thousands of people in developing nations access to affordable renewable energy.

Yes, our hair is more than just for fashion.

There are three transfer methods of energy that we need to understand: conduction, convection, and radiation. But, science has documented a fourth method and yes it has to do with HAIR! This process is call photosynthesis it is the process is when plants can store energy and use it for later it is directly connected to the color of the plant. Much like how our skin melanin is connected to helping us store the sun energy. I personally believe this is the reason people with lots of melanin in the skin age slower. I believe we are storing energy in our skin cells and using it at a rapid rate to repair our aging skin therefore causing us to look much younger. Hence the phrase, *black don't crack*.

Conduction:

Heat is thermal energy and in solids, it can be transferred by conduction. Thermal energy like how we snuggle together to get body heat form, one person, when we're cold. Heat is passed along from the hotter end of an object to the cold end by the particles in the solid vibrating. Hotter particles vibrate fast and cause the particles next to them to vibrate as they gain heat energy too. Solids conduct heat due to how tightly packed their particles are.

Convection:

Fluids, that is both gases and liquids, can transfer heat energy by convection. It is easiest to explain this while thinking of an example: Imagine a beaker of water being heated from the bottom. As the water particles at the bottom get hot, they expand and become less dense. This means they will rise to the top of the beaker, and other colder water particles will fall to replace them. After a while, the 'new' cold particles at the bottom will be heated and they will then rise to the top as they will be less dense. The water at the top which was first heated will have slightly cooled by then, so will sink down to the bottom, but then will be reheated and the same process will happen again.

This constant flow of the fluid due to the expansion/ change in density of the particles is called a convection current. Over time all the fluid reaches a constant temperature.

Radiation:

Radiation is different from the other two processes as it doesn't require particles in its transfer of energy. Instead, infra-red radiation is a type of electromagnetic radiation. This means that the energy is transferred by waves rather than particles. Radiation is how we feel the heat from the sun on Earth, as waves can pass through the vacuum of space where there are no particles.

When we talk about Radiation understand we have now just entered the world of waves. Airwaves, microwaves, Infrared waves etc. There is a great chart to help you visualize the waves of energy.

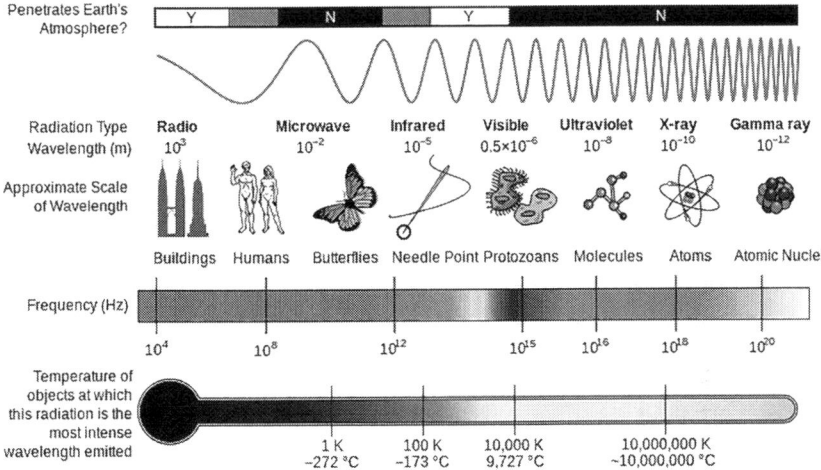

Notice how all the wavelengths look like an ocean but the higher the waves go the less energy it takes. Well, that is because it moves slower, therefore, it takes less energy. Ultraviolet waves and X-rays take a lot of energy and they both can be considered dangers to us as well.

Nuclear fusion converts hydrogen atoms into helium. The by-product of nuclear fusion in the Sun's core is a massive volume of energy that gets released and radiates outward toward the surface of the Sun and then into the solar system beyond it.

Photosynthesis

Plants, as well as some bacteria and protistans, undergo a process called photosynthesis in order to use the energy from sunlight to produce glucose from carbon dioxide and water. This glucose can be converted into pyruvate which releases adenosine triphosphate (ATP) by cellular respiration. Oxygen is also formed. Photosynthesis may be summarized by the word equation: carbon dioxide plus water leads to glucose and oxygen and water.

Blah, blah, blah, whatever, all that science talk. What I am saying is the sun is making energy that we are using that comes from even beyond our planet earth. Now, think about it we are absorbing the unaversive in our body and we need it to function. Even the food we eat are literally atoms of energy that is what we called calories. You absorb energy from the sun and use it as calories. You can also eat energy and use it for calories, but it is the same energy and you need this in your body to function. Your hair helps you to absorb the energy around you. The energy you take in from the sun can work as a conductor and the melanin in your hair can help to hold and store this energy for later use. This is the reason why the longer and thicker your hair is the more you want to pin it up and keep it off your shoulders on a hot day. Because your hair can become a magnet to energy and generate heat.

The greater the energy, the larger the frequency and the shorter (smaller) the wavelength. Given the relationship between wavelength and frequency—the higher the frequency, the shorter the wavelength—it follows that short wavelengths are more energetic than long wavelengths.

Frequency is the rate of vibration and oscillation measured over a specific period of time (usually one second). The greater the energy, the larger the frequency and the shorter (smaller) the wavelength. This is why someone with a stronger energy, whether negative or positive, can enter a room and affect the mood of a room.

The organs and tissues are made of cells, which are made of molecules, which are atoms. Atoms are made of subatomic particles which are energy! That is why science says, "everything is energy." Understanding this can help you to find the frequency of money and better health which can also help you to understand why you tend to lose money fast or always attract health problems. Your hair can harness the energy directly from the sun. This energy possesses great power that is directly connected to our health. If we understand how to utilize its power, we can't help but enhance our health and financial wealth.

When trying to comprehend the connection between your hair and your money remember this: energy= frequency= vibrations. Everything on our universe vibrates at a frequency including money. Don't think of wealth in the terms of physical money since money is only paper. Think more about what things you would like or could do with the actual money. For example, if one of the reasons you want money is to buy a luxury car think about that vehicle, think about being able to acquire it and think about how it would make you feel to have it.

CHAPTER 18

Match the Frequency

"If you want to find the secrets of the universe, think in terms of energy, frequency and vibration."
~ Nikola Tesla

Are You Negative or Positive?

*H*ave you ever heard people speak and say you could create the reality you live in or the experience you are having is because you have attracted it? Doesn't it sound like BS to the 9th power? Well, perhaps there is something to it.

I have found that it is possible to attract your ideal reality. This process can take years for you to match the frequency strong enough. I remember charting my personal life desires. During this process, I noticed that there was a 7-year difference from when I would focus on a dream before I would see the manifestation of it taking place. Over time, I learned ways to successfully shorten that time.

The first time I decided to do a life chart was after watching the Oprah Winfrey show. Her guest was a comedian who shared a story about how he wrote a 10 million dollars check to himself and kept it in his wallet. The check had gotten so old but 10 years later one day the first big project he had ever done paid him 10 million dollars. It immediately connected me to an old memory from when I was a little girl on the island. I would walk barefooted in the sands with my cousin, Josephine, just talking and laughing. I would tell her that I was going to be a movie star. You have to understand why this was so deep. I lived on a little island in the VI and had never even been to the movies to be able to understand what a movie star was. Yet, I would tell her and only her over and over again all about how I was going to be in a movie. Then some way somehow, I ended up moving to California and as a little homeless girl auditioning for the starring role in Hollywood for a Steven Spielberg film. The movie was already cast and Whoopie Goldberg was assured the leading role but the universe said, wait a minute. I didn't even have an agent, never been to an audition but everything had aligned and destiny played its part.

When I look back there were more moments like that although my life. That's when I realized you don't need to know anything. You don't need to have all these things they tell you is required for success like a college degree, contacts, wealthy friends. What you need is to be able to harness a level of power within your self. To become a force of energy that can bend and change the current reality! But in order to do that, you must hold that type of positive energy within you and it starts with how you feel about yourself. Because if you feel negative about yourself you will bring more negative people, experiances and situations into your life.

Change literally starts in the head. You have to truly feel positive and good about yourself. You could give lectures and talk all day on social media about how wonderful you life is but if you truly don't feel good about it your life will reflect it. You can't fool energy. How long it takes for you to receive back the energy you give out depends on how powerful your frequency is within the universe. Your hair can then hold the energy you harness and make it readily available to use and the color of your hair is what will determine how much energy you can harness. YES, that color black is the strongest color to hold the sun's energy. Therefore, if someone wanted for you to attract more bad or self-destructive things in your life all that would need is for you to believe and feel bad about yourself. How you feel about yourself in your own mind will naturally over time manifest into a reality. We live in a society that teaches us to be quick to complain, give a review, and let others know how you feel. Yet, we are only quick to share negative things. We don't understand that the more you focus your energy to say anything negative or to stay in that negative space the more your mind becomes mentally trained to only see negativity and problems. Consequently, you attract more of the same experiences.

Here's a challenge for you. For 30 days, try to only speak, share or write about what is good. It could be fun to try it out. Let's say your car got repossessed—good, now I don't have any more car payments. Your boss says there is no overtime this week—great, now I get to spend a little extra time with the family. Now, I know it is impossible to not ever have a complaint or need time to vent some of the negative energy or stupidity you come across. I use only one or two people in my life for that sounding board. They are great at allowing me to not only release that energy but more importantly to move on. I say release because energy can not be created or destroyed, only transferred. Therefore whenever someone gives me to much negative energy or I have collected an ample amount over the week; I usually release it by meditating, exercising, or venting.

As I studied, I increasingly found that the color of your hair and skin can help to increase your universal energy and power. Your thoughts and intentions can have a higher impact in the universe simply by the color of your hair and skin. When I discovered that I thought: wow, imagine if you thought of yourself as very low and not worthy of much? How much power can you send into the universe?

Think about it, we all know some basic science and physics right? Dark colors attract more heat and sunlight. But let's go deeper than that. Heat and light are both different types of energy. Light energy can be converted into heat energy. A black object absorbs all wavelengths of light and converts them into heat, so the object gets warm. A white object reflects all wavelengths of light, so the light is not converted into heat and the temperature of the object does not noticeably increase.

Different wavelengths (colors) of light have different amounts of energy. Violet light has more energy than red light. If we compare an object that absorbs violet light with an object that absorbs the same number of photons (particles of light) of red light, then the object that absorbs violet light will absorb more heat than the object that absorbs red light.

The amount of heat absorbed is also affected by how light or dark an object is. A dark object of a given color will absorb more photons than a light object of the same color, so it will absorb more heat and get warmer. If something has the capability (because of its color) to attract more energy that means it has the capability to have more power. Remember the greater the energy, the larger the frequency and the shorter (smaller) the wavelength. The higher the frequency, the shorter the wavelength. Shorter wavelengths (and higher frequencies) also have more energy, so types of light like gamma rays, X-rays, and ultraviolet light are more energetic than visible light. Infrared, microwaves and radio waves are less energetic than the light in the visible spectrum.

Basically, darker color attracts more heat and energy and it is the number one reason I love to wear my hair in extra-long thick twisted black braids whenever I am going through deep mediational time periods in which I am trying to harness extra power to channel my desires into the universe. It is no accident I wear my hair a particular way. For example, I don't wear wigs because I want my scalp to get as much natural light as possible, so it can directly absorb into my cells. I wear my own hair out during resting periods like when on vacation or I have long periods of down time because less hair on my head allows me not to do too much deep thinking. I am pulling less of the universal energy towards me therefore, I can be more carefree.

This explains on a more scientific level why when you are depressed just simply getting your hair done can give you me more energy and make you feel good. Or why when you cut your hair, you can feel like you release stress, or a weight has been lifted. Your hair is directly connected to your feelings, your mental health and physical health.

Hair Color and Wealth

You may believe that your black hair is common and not as unique as other colors such as red, or blond, but it is the color black that the universe needs. Statistically, about 95% of the world has black hair and this includes some forms of brown hair that are still considered in the darker hues and labeled as black. It's the same logic for why the abundance of air on earth does not make air not valuable. Once you understand the value of your black hair and how it works within the solar system then you will understand its value and commonality.

The products and maintenance you use to care for your hair should be regarded with extreme care and importance. For this is the stabilizer and conductor for your body's overall health. When you understand what they understand about hair then it all would make sense why laws would be enforced to control how you wear your hair and care for your hair. Why would you be required to shave your hair or beard to become part of a structural organization? Why would you be required to cover your hair? Why would products be made that would cause destruction to your hair? Why is the black hair industry an 800-billion-dollar industry, while Caucasian hair products are only a third of that? If you are not able to answer these questions after reading this book, then read the book again.

Your belief that it is just hair is why you don't believe in the power of self and the reason you lack the power of wealth. Take the Jewish community for example. The power of their wealth has very little to do with money but with their self-awareness of love for themselves and others. It is actually required for their young to learn their past history and value of self-early in life. They are not reminded of their past history as a form of insult or shame for being enslaved but as a reminder of how resilient they were as a people to survive with all odds against them.

They have set routines and a heritage they teach their children. The routine is taught around the same time to each child. You may only know of a few like the Bar Mitzvah, the religious initiation ceremony of a Jewish boy who has reached the age of 13 and is regarded as ready to observe religious precepts and eligible to take part in public worship. But did you also know, they train their children about money management at a very young age? They instill these teachings the same way around the same time of a child's life because it is the age when they are most teachable.

In one teaching, they use five jars, each jar is labeled and has an opening at the top. The jar is equivalent to what we may call a piggy bank. The jars are labeled *tithe, giving & offering, saving, investing* and *spending*. Let's say a child is given 10 Shekels (Israeli Currency), the child is expected to put one Shekel in the Jar labeled *tithe*, another Shekel in the giving & offering jar, another Shekel in the *savings* jar, two Shekels in the *investing* jar and the last *spending* jar receives the remaining five Shekels. The child is then only allowed to open the *giving* jar on Sundays, while the *tithe* jar is opened on at the end of the month.

For myself at a young age no one taught me about money, luckily as a young child, I was fortunate enough to spend time around millionaires and billionaires.

To put it simply, the color of your skin is directly connected to the universe and you are what it needs to exist. Your black hair color is a special conductor used to ground you because of the extreme energy and power your body must process. The universe does not see you as a black person, a Jewish person, Latin, Mexican, an immigrant or any label. It only knows you as an element on the planet. It knows only how many atoms your body contains and how fast it communicates to it. It is responding to the frequency it hears. The greater power of energy you hold, the more it speaks to the universe with greater volumes and swiftness. Therefore, be careful of the people you spend time with, for they feed your thoughts. Be careful of the books you read, for they imprint your mind. Be careful of the products you use, because they invade your body and be careful of the things you speak because your voice speaks with frequency.

> *"The conspiracy was for you to think it was just hair but it is NOT JUST HAIR."*
> ~ Desreta Jackson

CHAPTER 19

Topics and Questions Discussion

*"One good conversation can shift the
direction of change forever."*
~ Linda Lambert

Topics and Questions

Below are list of relevant topics and questions meant to continue the conversation and help search for deeper truths.

Topics

- The Big Bang Theory vs. Creation
- Darwinism
- Hair Culture
- Good hair vs. Bad hair
- General Sherman T. Sherman's middle name "Tecumseh"
- What do you think the author meant by the title The Black Hair Conspiracy?

Questions

1. Is there a lack of information regarding proper hair care especially information about African-American hair care?
2. Is there a flood of misinformation regarding proper hair care especially information about African-American hair care?
3. Do social media sites and hair media influencers do more harm or good for the general public?
4. How does the media influence the perspective of different hair types?

How to Order BlackSilk Products

*T*he full Silk Hair Growth System can be ordered online at MyBlackSilk.com.

Along with various of hair and skin products that all natural and low chemically designed.

Follow us on Facebook, Twitter, and Instagram.

Facebook: @BlackSilk Products
Twitter: @BlackSilkxhair
Instagram: @blacksilkproducts

For appearances, speaking engagements and book signings for Ms. Desreta contact islandmanagement@rocketmail.com.

Bibliography

Aalborg, Jenny, Joseph G. Morelli, Tim E. Byers, Stefan T. Mokrohisky, and Lori A. Crane. "Effect Of Hair Color And Sun Sensitivity On Nevus Counts In White Children In Colorado". Journal Of The American Academy Of Dermatology 63, no. 3 (September 2010): 430-439. doi:10.1016/ j.jaad. 2009.10.011.

Anderson, Claud. *Dirty Little Secrets about Black History, Its Heroes, and Other Troublemakers.* PowerNomics Corporation of America, 2007.

Brady, Mathew. *The Photography Book.* London: Phaidon Press. 1997.

J, Kelly. "How to Balance PH in Hair Naturally." *HOW TO BALANCE PH IN HAIR NATURALLY,* Natural Girls Rock, 2018, www.naturalgirlsrock.com/blogs/rockin-guest-bloggers-speak/12212729-how-to-balance-ph-in-hair-naturally.

"Legacy." Merriam-Webster, Merriam-Webster, 17 July 2018, www.merriam-webster.com/dictionary/legacy.

Mwema, Zack. 2013. "WHAT THE JEWS TEACH THEIR CHILDREN ABOUT MONEY". Blog. STARS OF THE FUTURE. http://smartmoneymanagers.blogspot.com/2013/07/what-jews-teach-their-children-bout.html.

Olson, Samantha. "8 Ways Having Red Hair Affects A Person's Health, From Pain To Sex" last modified August 18, 2015. https://www.medicaldaily.com/8-ways-having-red-hair-affects-persons health-pain-sex-348198

Sherman, William T. *Memoirs of Gen. William T. Sherman.* (2). New York: D. Appleton and Company. 2012.

"Why Do Black Objects Absorb More Heat (Light) than Lighter Colored Objects? What Do Wavelengths Have to Do with It?" *UCSB Science Line*, National Science Foundation and UCSB School-University Partnership, 2013, scienceline.ucsb.edu/get-key.php?key=3873.

Wikipedia contributors, "1992 Los Angeles riots," Wikipedia, The Free Encyclopedia, https://en.wikipedia.org/w/index.php?title=1992_Los_Angeles_riots&oldid=851235562

Wikipedia contributors, "Special Field Orders No. 15," Wikipedia, The Free Encyclopedia, https://en.wikipedia.org/w/index.php?title=Special_Field_Orders_No._15&oldid=848393908

Made in the USA
Columbia, SC
30 September 2021